HORSING ABOUT WITH DOGS & LORRIES

HORSING ABOUT WITH DOGS & LORRIES

The Autobiography
of a
Countrywoman of Character

Joan Newell

MALVERN
MMXII

HORSING ABOUT WITH DOGS AND LORRIES

First published in 2012 by
JRB Publishing

ISBN 978-0-9566403-5-2

Designed by **JRB**

john@jrbpub.net

Printed & Bound in Great Britain by **Aspect Design**, Malvern

www.aspect-design.net

Dedicated to my
Friend and Partner

Joan Bradshaw

CONTENTS

Appendices

THANKS TO:

Gill Ferris
  - for transcribing the WI Talks from tape to computer, typing, and for proof-reading too.

Cath Lockley; Rosemary McCullock; Rosie McCarry; Russell Taylor; Meriel Bennett
  - for telling tales and filling in gaps.

Carol Nicholls
  - for recalling some of our experiences and for hosting the Book Launch at The Nursery on Saturday 20th October, 2012.

John Horton
  - for his kind words in the Foreword, the wonderful original paintings for the Front & Rear Covers and their further use throughout.

Peter Livesley
  - for his pencil drawing of Grange Farm house on page 135.

Mo Bradshaw
  - for final proof reading.

Photographs and illustrations have been acknowledged where at all possible.

FOREWORD

The trip to Skomer Island in Pembrokeshire turned from a walk through a carpet of bluebells in the warm June sunshine to a ten degree drop in temperature and our being engulfed in a mighty squall of high wind and horizontal rain, when we were about as far from the boat as we could be.   It was at this point that an only slightly breathless Joan reminded us that –
"I am nearly eighty you know!" - and that was ten years ago…..
The day ended happily with hot soup and a chance to change clothes at a local cafe back on the mainland, followed up by a whisky-mac on the way home, which prompted more stories from Joan.

This description exemplifies Joan's stoical approach to life coloured with a down-to-earth sense of humour and a passion for the countryside and natural world in all its forms.

We've taken many short breaks away with Joan to all corners of the British Isles, seeking out the best that the landscape and natural flora and fauna has to offer and have enjoyed her company immensely as she has recounted tales from such a rich and varied life. A life ranging from her childhood growing up in Worcestershire; early wartime experiences in the Army; running the farm with cattle, horses and dogs; driving scientists around the country; through to creating and developing the nursery at Grange Farm. All recalled with great fondness and good humour, so how wonderful it is that these memories and experiences are now recorded here for posterity.

Here is the full and interesting life of a warm, kind and entertaining character who draws the best from her fellow human beings.

John and Barbara Horton
March 2012

INTRODUCTION

After the persuasion and encouragement of John Bradshaw, I have finally written this book for a particular purpose. Younger readers, particularly women who today have so much freedom and autonomy, will not be aware of the struggle life was in the late 1940's and early 1950's for women who did not conform to society's expectations. Some men thought that, after the war, women should crawl back into their shells and keep quiet. However, I am pleased to say that they had a nasty shock as many women continued to do their own thing. (By the way, I do like men too and have had and still have many male friends.)

Joan and I were repeatedly told that we would never make a go of it and were quite mad - which made us all the more determined!

So, the hedge we laid is still there, the barn is still standing and the nursery we created is going from strength to strength.....

Jo Newell
September 2012

Chapter 1
WHERE IT ALL BEGAN

Childhood

I was born at around midnight, so it was on either Sunday 8th April or Monday 9th in 1923. My father says it was on the 9th, because that was his birthday. He was out in the back garden, with his pal Gil, puffing on their pipes when they heard my first yell.

"Ah – the bugger'll be a boy then. No girl would ever be that loud!"

However, my mother, who was actually there at the time, said it was on the 8th, because that was her birthday.

I'm not even sure whether I was actually born in Woodmancote, up on Cleeve Hill, or in Bishops Cleeve itself. Certainly I was christened at Bishops Cleeve Church, as 'Dorothy Joan Newell'. However, after I left the Army and met Joan Bradshaw, I was often called 'Jo', although not always.

My father, Thomas Charles Percival Newell, was a butcher and my first real memory is of being taken in the butcher's cart, which I thought was great because, from as far back as I can remember, I loved horses. He always had a smart horse, being a horse lover himself. And that is my earliest memory: the thrill of being with horses.

Once, so my father told me, he was looking for me all over the place and he finally found me in the stable, with my arms hugging the horse's hind leg, with my head on his hock, and quietly singing.....
I don't really remember it myself, but I'm sure it's true.

As I got older and bigger, I was allowed to take the reins and I thought I was really something - talk about being on cloud nine! I was very close to my father and can remember sneaking into his bed early in the morning and getting him to scratch my back for me.

"Only a hundred, Dad" and then I'd start counting, very very slowly.....

*I can find no photographs of myself
with horses from my childhood days,
just this one of me sitting on
Auntie Evelyn's boyfriend's motorcycle.*

Some friends of my father, Mr. & Mrs. Adcock, whom I knew as Uncle Gil and Aunty Doll, had a farm in Prestbury village and my greatest joy was to go and stay there with them. Uncle Gil had been given a chaser, a retired steeple-chaser, and we used to ride him up on the hill. However, my Uncle would never let us have a saddle, because of the risk that we'd get a foot caught in the stirrup and get dragged. So we rode him bare back, which taught us how to stay on. By the time we'd fallen off and chased the old horse half way over Cleeve Hill, we soon learned how to stay on. I still think that the best way to learn to ride is bare back, and many years later I taught my friend Rosie to ride, starting her without a saddle.

I think it was that which instilled in me my love of the countryside and farming. Really, all I ever wanted to do was either be with horses or on a farm - and that went on for many years.

The Adcocks had four children: Bob who was my age, we were the eldest two, and then they had the twins Billy & Mary, and then there was the young one, Michael, who was the baby, and we all looked after him. We had terrific times there. It shows you how times have changed because sometimes Uncle Gil would say *"I want you kids to go up on the hill and count the cattle and the sheep"*. That would be on Cleeve Hill, and they'd be all over it and Prestbury Hill too, and so off we'd go. Aunty Doll would cut us a big hunk of bread and cheese, and a piece of fruit cake too, and off we'd go. We'd be up there all day, all on our own. We were just little kids, about seven or so, going and spending the whole day up there. There was a pool where we used to swim, and we'd drink from the little streams running into it. I wouldn't dare do that now.

The farm next to Uncle Gil's had a really good apple orchard and we used to go scrumping there. I suppose we weren't very careful about it and the farmer, who was a friend of Uncle Gil's, soon saw what was happening. So he came out shouting at us and fired his shotgun up into the air. That got us running I can tell you – we were really scared! But I expect him and Uncle Gil had a good laugh about it over a pint of cider or two. Uncle Gil walked with a limp and he'd have come out, wearing his knee-britches and khaki smock as he always did, and waving his walking stick at us, with his usual phrase *"You little buggers – get off, get away with you!"* - but the shotgun had more effect on us.

Nobody had a laugh about what happened to poor old Michael, though. When we were all out in the lanes nearby, some local boys would sometimes hide behind a wall and then throw stones at us. Now, we weren't going to just take it so we threw stones back at them, didn't we? The bad thing was that eventually one of us got hurt and it was Michael that got cut right across the bridge of his nose by a bit of glass. His nose was hanging down over his lip! He got back to Aunty Doll, his mum, and she pushed it back up into place, wrapped a towel round it and then took him to the hospital. No telephones, cars or taxis, they just walked the mile to the bus stop and caught a bus to Cheltenham General Hospital where they sewed it up. He had the scar across the top his nose ever after.

I'm afraid that 'ever after' wasn't too long though. Michael was a dispatch rider in the army during the war, and he had some sort of an accident – I don't know quite what. Anyway, he'd hurt his head in the accident and suffered from a permanent bad headache. It seems that the pain was so bad and so permanent that, very shortly after the war, he just had to finish it and he shot himself.

Some more friends of my parents were Mr & Mrs Jeynes who lived at Bishops Cleeve. George Jeynes worked on the railway and was about medium size with a moustache and a lovely friendly smile. His wife was very tall – at least that's how I remember her. They had a lovely Cotswold stone cottage with outbuildings and a long garden. He loved his garden and it had rows and rows of vegetables all the way down. There were a few flowers too, but just for Mrs.

Jeynes to brighten the cottage up. Right down at the bottom of the garden was an orchard, with a pigsty there too, where he kept one or two pigs.

They had two boys, and I think it was George who worked for my father in his butchers shop. But then I used to help him in the shop too. On a Saturday I'd get up early and have a cup of tea in the kitchen with him, just the two of us, I enjoyed that. Then we'd go into the shop and I'd help him bone the meat and put the orders up for the day. So there I was, a little girl, surrounded by big, very sharp knives, choppers and saws. 'Health & Safety'? Never heard of it! However, I did cut myself badly once, right down to the bone and I could see it, all white and shiny. My mother took me to the chemist – a doctor would have been too expensive – and the chemist poured yellow iodine onto it. That made me sit up – and learn not to cut myself again!

I used to love visiting Mr & Mrs Jeynes because I was always made a fuss of, and they had a lovely big kitchen with a range. On top of the range there was often a big jug of cider – warm cider might sound rather strange nowadays, but they used to quench a red hot poker in it – which made it taste wonderful – and probably killed most of the alcohol for us kids.

I remember my Dad telling me that, when I was about four years old, I'd gone down Mr. Jeynes garden all on my own, collecting all his labels from the end of each row of recently planted seeds - so he had no idea what was where! But I didn't get tanned for it – I suppose I could do no wrong in their eyes, for some now unknown reason.

I carried on visiting Mr. & Mrs Jeynes for many years, and not only because we'd always return home with a basket full of fresh vegetables and home-cured bacon, but because I was really very fond of them and they were wonderful friends.

Many years later I took Joan over there to meet them and of course we all got on very well. I wish I hadn't gone back after that though, because after Mr. & Mrs. Jeynes passed on, the place was sold and the lovely cottage was completely demolished. The site, and the orchard and all of his garden too, was built on with an estate of totally characterless modern bungalows. Hideous they were, little boxes. Mind you, it wasn't just there that the vandals had their way. The Adcocks' farm at Prestbury went the same way, as did many other fine buildings in the 1960s.

A Family Gathering.
From left to right: Uncle Arthur with Gran's dog, Bob; Auntie Dixie; Gran Newell; Joan Newell; Dad (Tom); Auntie Lil; Mum (Dot); Auntie Evelyn.   Uncle Fred wasn't there that day.

3

But going back to happier days, sometimes we'd take back a bunch of wild flowers for Aunty Doll - but I suppose you aren't allowed to do that now either. And you certainly wouldn't dare let kids go out on their own nowadays, would you?
But then, at school I was hit hard on each hand with a stick for bad handwriting, and kids don't get that now either, do they? It was a different world then.

I think children nowadays are deprived of a lot of things that are important in life. Sitting in front of the goggle-box is one of the worst things they can do, I think. And looking at these video games and things like that, they're not having fun, are they?
Oh, they've got a lot of things that we didn't have, but I don't think that's necessarily good for them. I think they have too much, too soon. Far too much, and I think the pocket money that some of them get is ridiculous! I think children have got to learn the value of money, right from the word go. Otherwise they expect too much and they get greedy. That is the trouble with people nowadays isn't it, they're too greedy!

Anyway, I was only really interested in the countryside and I loved animals, and dogs and horses. They've been a big part of my life all through and I couldn't envisage a life where I didn't have horses and dogs. I've never ever been without a dog for long, except when I was in the army, and there's not been much of my life without a horse either.

Harborne College

But then my father, against his will and my mother's too I think, and certainly against my wishes, was persuaded by his brother to move to Bourneville, near Birmingham - which we all hated. I went to school there of course, but fortunately for me my parents, at great sacrifice, sent me to a private school, Harborne College*. Whatever your feelings may be, I think it was good for me - certainly in those days. For one thing it prevented me from ever having a Birmingham accent because I had to have elocution lessons.

Our uniform was a maroon blazer, black gymslip, cream collared blouse, with a maroon, blue and cream striped tie and hatband. In summer we wore a Panama or a beret with the HC badge, and in winter a black velour hat, with the coloured band around.
We had a Morning Assembly each day, with prayers, but they didn't make a big thing about it. Dress, presentation, manners, speech and diction – these were the things that mattered. I enjoyed English, History and Geography, but not much else – I was never one for studying.

---

* Harborne College
In the 1930s, Harborne College was located in Leighton House, on Hagley Road in Edgbaston. It was an all-girls school, with classrooms in the main house and others behind in a more recently built classroom-block. There were no science laboratories or facilities, but there was a well-equipped gymnasium because sports and gymnastics were high on the school's curriculum. The small playground was discretely located at the back.
The senior staff included three sisters: the headmistress of the Higher School was Miss Kathleen Lee, whose enthusiasm and qualifications were centred on Physical Education. Her sister, Mrs Wurth, taught German, being married to a German gentleman, and so she insisted in being addressed as 'Frau Wurth'. A third sister was the headmistress of the Lower School and is remembered as being a particularly pleasant person.
The curriculum included English, French, German, Elocution, Arithmetic, History, Geography, Religious Education and P.E., but apparently no Sciences at all. Presumably as a result, Harbourne College could not offer any formal qualifications, such as Matriculation, which required a pass in a set of subjects including Science. The college did, however, prepare girls for Society.
The school closed in 1941, but Leighton House was taken over in 1943 by St.Philip's RC Grammar School as its Independent Preparatory School, until 1976. At the time of writing, the building is derelict and abandoned.

I did enjoy PE though, especially hockey, tennis, netball and cricket. One year I was the youngest in the Hockey First Eleven, and had to go up onto the stage during assembly to receive the team badge.

"If only you were as good at your studies as you are at games, my girl, you'd be our star pupil!" I remember that Miss Lee said to me.   Oh well.

I was there for about six years, I suppose, but before I'd left school, my family moved back to the countryside, near Malvern, where my father continued in business. I could have left at 14, but my father had insisted that I should stay on for another year, so I had to stay with my father's brother and his wife, Uncle Arthur and Auntie Marjorie, who was a hairdresser. They were all right, but Auntie Marjorie's aged mother who lived with them was a real old bat, and she made my life awful while I was there. I don't know why my father made me stay on – I still got no qualifications and it was just a waste of his money and my time, but in those days you did what you were told. However, I made some good friends there, one of whom, Barbara Bishop, I still keep in touch with to this day.

So, I caught the bus to Malvern each Friday evening and returned to Birmingham each Monday morning. Over the weekends, I did visit my Auntie at Upton and sometimes rode Ronnie Vines' horse – and that was the best bit of the whole of my week!

Leaving School

I left school at 15 and went to work with horses, as a 'working pupil' with the two ladies at the small Riding School in Lower Howsell. It was rather a funny set-up really. They were very <u>very</u> prim and proper and I really had to mind my p's and q's. They didn't teach me an awful lot, but I quite enjoyed my stay there.

However, my mother then found me a 'proper' job, as a Milliner's Assistant at Cox & Painter's, in Warwick House on Wells Road in Malvern. Unsurprisingly this didn't appeal to me at all. But there I was, in the hats department, doing…. Well, I don't know quite what I was doing really, just looking out of the window most of the time, wishing I was on the back of horse and a long way off, I expect.

One day though, I was walking along a corridor and found myself passing the Managing Director's office and I just turned, knocked, and went in. There he was, sitting behind his big desk - I'd never spoken to him before of course, because he was 'up there', beyond reach, and he certainly wouldn't deign to speak to a mere 16 year old girl in the Millinery Department.

"Hello. And what do you want?" was all he said. Looking back at it, I'm amazed that I wasn't tongue-tied at that point, but no, I told him that I didn't like hats and wanted to be in the Sports Department. I can't remember quite what he said then, something to the effect that he'd see what could be done, but he wasn't at all how I expected him to be, he was really quite nice and friendly. But, when word got down to the department about what I'd done, I was really hauled over the coals by the Buyer and the Sales Girl. Oh I'd really done it – I had ignored The System and, insultingly, had by-passed my superiors and immediate bosses.   Their only consolation was that I hadn't got my own way and for me the Sports Department remained the slightly greener grass on the other side of the fence. But in fact it wasn't as bad as all that because they were quite nice people really and as well as feeling slighted they found it quite funny too.

In fact, a while later, when I had left Cox & Painters and was working with horses again, the Buyer passed by and stopped to talk to me.

"This is much more your cup of tea, isn't it, Joan?" she said, smiling. She was right.

After about six months of boredom at the shop, I saw an advert in a window and got myself a far better job. My mother was of course horrified that, just on my own authority, I had left a good apprenticeship and gone to a job of much lower status. But at that point I think she gave up on me.

I'd got a job in Malvern doing a milk delivery, which was darned hard work! I had to be up there at five in the morning - but it was with horses so that was alright. I used to go up to the stables, feed the horse, groom him, tack him up, put him in the cart, take him down to the dairy, load up and off I used to set. If you know Malvern, all the way along the Wells Road you were either up hill and down again or down hill and up again, carrying heavy milk pails and such things, which was jolly hard work.

Anyway you got back to the dairy about 9 o'clock where the housekeeper used to cook us a most ginormous breakfast – egg, sausages, bacon and fried bread and tomatoes and anything that was going, and then toast and marmalade. That kept us going for the day! Then we used to set off again for the late morning round, which took us in the other direction in Malvern. Then we'd get back about 2 o'clock, put the horse to bed, groom him, feed him, clean the tack - and then you were finished for the day. So, back home I used to go - and I can't remember what I did then.... Slept I should think.

For my 17th birthday, my father, treated me to a course of driving lessons. This was quite wonderful in those days, because before the war girls didn't drive. Women didn't drive. In fact, nobody drove except the well off, or people who did it for a living.

Then I got a job as a van driver, with a baker who was a friend of my fathers. This was to get me some more experience in driving. That meant driving round Worcester, which I didn't like very much, but it paid quite well and my parents approved.

The Onset Of War

That all went on for some time and then one day in 1941 I happened to be in Worcester and I saw a convoy of Army lorries going through, all driven by girls.

I thought *'Ah, that's for me!'* So off I went to the Recruiting Office, all fired up and keen to join the ATS* - but I was only 17.

"You're too young, but we'll be in touch with you when you are 18" they said..

Come April and my birthday I was watching the post, and watching the post, and nothing came. Eventually in May it did come, and yet again, my father nearly had a fit when he saw it, and so did my mother. I was a real trial for them I suppose. Anyway, they eventually accepted the fact that I wanted to go, and they had a week to get used to it and for me to get ready - and off I went.

* **ATS** - the Auxiliary Territorial Service. Formed in 1938, combining the female members of the Territorial Army and the Women's Transport Service, thereafter including all women in the British Army, apart from nurses who were in QAIMS. Women serving in the ATS received two-thirds the pay of male soldiers.
In 1949, the ATS was merged into the WRAC, the Women's Royal Army Corps.

Chapter 2

A NEW FAMILY

Army Training

I joined up and volunteered as a driver. Of course, you had to be able to drive already, otherwise they wouldn't have you as a driver - because they certainly wouldn't teach you!

I went to Dering Lines Army Camp, near the town of Brecon, where I had six weeks of sheer misery.

I was going to be a driver, but instead of getting us used to lorries, we had a lot of square bashing, which gave us blisters on our heels. We had to wear starched collars, which gave us blisters on our necks. It was June and very hot, despite which we were taken on route marches.

The food was awful and we had all our jabs in one go, which made us feel ill.

Private D.J.Newell

Not only that, but we were hounded by the Redcaps. They were the Military Police and on the whole they were not very nice people at all. The Redcaps saw us as easy prey – those women enjoyed their job, y'know. They were out to get you and most of them were pretty unpleasant to be honest. As a result, everybody hated them and we used to bolt if we saw them coming, even if you hadn't done anything they could get you for.

We were all very glad to move away from there really.

But I do remember just one amusing incident. We weren't allowed in the pubs, they were strictly taboo, but the camp was on the railway line and there was a pub up the line, which we sometimes used to sneak off to. Not to drink a lot, for one thing we couldn't afford it, but to talk with the locals and the landlady used to cook us some supper – egg and bacon or something like that – real food! Some of it black market I'm sure.

Anyway one night Rita and I and a couple of others went up to the pub and shortly after we'd started tucking into a lovely supper, the locals came into the kitchen and said *"There's some Red-caps coming down the line"*. So the landlady said *"Come with me - I'll hide you"*.

So off down the garden we went and she hid us in the privy, which was very small, very hot and very smelly. There were about four of us crammed into this little hut with a peephole in the door.

We peeped through the hole and these two Redcaps came down the garden, admiring the flowers and all the vegetables that were growing in it.   We were praying that one of them didn't want to spend a penny! Anyway, eventually the landlady got rid of them and then came and knocked on the door and said that we could come out.   Of course by then all of us were collapsing with laughter and frightened to death in case we got caught - and glad to get back out into the fresh air!

Jo, Rita, Madge & Another

From there I went up to Bramcote, but in the meantime they did their best to persuade us to go onto Ack-Ack instead of driving.   There were three of us who wouldn't give in - we were determined to be drivers and we said we'd joined as drivers and we'd volunteered to be drivers and we wouldn't consider doing anything else.   So they couldn't really do much about it and gave in gracefully, and so off we went up to Chillwell nearby, which was a big army camp near Nottingham.   This is where we were finally sent on a course of driving – learning how to drive big lorries and all different sorts of vehicles, which was very different for all of us.   We had just a fortnight there, compared to the useless 6 weeks of square-bashing, but I also did a maintenance course while I was there.

The camp was at the top of a hill, a bit like a mini Church Street in Malvern, which is also very steep.   We were marched up and down there about four or five times a day sometimes, so I think by the end of the fortnight we were pretty fit.   We used to go out in the lorry, about six of us, travelling in the back when not driving.   We each had a time at the wheel and then we had a break, and then a bit more.   We used to stay out all day really and I enjoyed this of course.   We drove all round the Nottinghamshire countryside, stopping for a cup of tea or coffee somewhere, before having our packed lunches at about midday.   Then we'd stop and have a cup of tea in the afternoon as well - the instructor was really quite a nice chap really.

At the end of the course we had to take a test, which we all passed because it was quite simple really.

And then we were posted.

Another, Jo, Rita & Madge

8

First Posting

Fortunately I was sent only as far away as Harlescott*, in Shrewsbury and were put into private billets, which we thought *"Oh great!"*. But it wasn't so great really. I was billeted with two ladies, Miss Morris and her housekeeper. The Morrises were THE family in Shrewsbury at the time. They had a big store and they had a big oil company and so the Morrises were quite a wealthy family. You can still buy Morris Oils today, I think. Anyway, it was nice house, but she was….. well, to me she seemed ancient! I suppose she must have been about 70 and dressed in a long black skirt with a black blouse, hair severely back in a bun - and her housekeeper ditto, even <u>older</u> I think. They really didn't approve of girls in uniform at all, which they made quite obvious, and so I thought it was ridiculous to park an Army girl there with them, who was going to be out all hours of the day and night and having to set off at any hour in the morning.

I could have to get up at 5 o'clock, 6 o'clock or 7 o'clock in the morning and not get back until 10, 11 or 12 o'clock at night – or even sometimes 2, 3 or 5 o'clock in the morning!

We were doing convoy duty, which involved picking up lorries from factories and taking them to various depots and then coming back by train, or to our own depot which of course meant an early night. But coming back from other places, with the trains as they were in wartime, was very hit and miss. What's more, if we were off on convoy we could be going anywhere and we'd be away for over-nights sometimes. We'd often go up to Scotland and then we'd be away two nights. We'd drive up and deliver the trucks to the docks probably. We did a lot of that, where they would be put on a ship to go abroad and then we'd come back on the train and sometimes we got back to Shrewsbury at 5pm - and sometimes we didn't.

Private billets were supposed to give us a meal when we came back. Well, you can imagine how that turned out, can't you? I mean, these two dear old ladies thought that they knew that I was supposed to be in at 10 o'clock at night and they could not understand why I wasn't in at the right time every night when I was on duty. In fact, the rule was 10 o'clock when <u>not</u> on duty – which wasn't much of the time. Also they certainly couldn't understand me having to get up at 5 o'clock and have my breakfast. They used to feed me in a little room in the front with a one bar electric fire - and it was perishing cold. It was very difficult for them - I mean these two ladies they must have wondered what had hit them! Anyway I didn't stay there long, obviously they couldn't accept it at all.

I next went to a family where the woman's husband was in the RAF and stationed locally at RAF Shawbury, so he was able to come home. They'd got 5 kids and it was all such a complete contrast! It was free and easy - she didn't mind the hours at all, she just said *"Oh well…"* and just gave me a key and that was that. I could come and go as I pleased and she didn't care what time I came in, on or off duty. I mean, her husband used to come home at all hours so she was used to it. Much more sensible. I was very happy there and we became great friends. The only thing was that I had to be careful when I came home and make a lot of noise, because sometimes she and her husband would be practising their 'rights' on the mat in front of the fire. So I used to come in whistling and banging about a bit you know, which was all quite amusing.

They were great people and I fed very well there too of course – it seemed that the bigger the family in war-time the better you eat because you had more to cope with. With rations, their mother could lump it all together and make something that would go further - and she was a good cook.

*__Harlescott VRD__ (Vehicle Reserve Depot) had recently been taken over by the Army from the RAF. It used to be RAF MTD, Harlescott (Motor Transport Depot), supporting the nearby aerodromes RAF Shawbury and RAF Turnhill.

Cound Hall

Overall, I think they had such a lot of difficulty with our irregular hours in private billets that they eventually took over a place called Cound Hall*, which is about 9 miles out of Shrewsbury. It had belonged to the McCorquodales, but they'd lost it by then of course.

It was a really beautiful place with lovely grounds and a huge lake and you could walk all round it. I was up on the top floor and there was a balcony outside and we could go out on the balcony and you looked all over the grounds, up to the pool and in the spring there were beautiful trees full of blossom and acres of daffodils. It was all wonderful, I thought.

I've called once or twice when I've gone by, but in 1997 I was with my cousin, Chris Cox and his wife Margaret, and we were passing so we stopped there.

We'd just parked and almost immediately a lady drew up in a car and asked if she could help us? It turned out to be the current owner of the place, a very friendly lady. She was interested to hear that I'd been stationed there during the war, so she showed us all over the place. I even went up all the many stairs to the very room where I had lived for about four years. That bit hadn't been restored at that point, but it brought many memories flooding back to me.

The wide stairs leading to grand front doors in particular reminded me of us all lining up in our Sections, first thing in the morning. We would salute and then be told to "*Stand Easy*" and be given orders and destinations for the day. Then we'd turn and march off to go and drive convoys of brand new trucks to far off distant ports.......

Jo revisiting Cound Hall in 1997

*Cound Hall. Built in 1703, in the Baroque style, from red brick and stone, featuring Corinthian pilasters and a unique C18 staircase. In the 1930s it was where the young Barbara Cartland lived whilst married to Alexander McCorquodale.

By the 1980s, however, it was vacant and in disrepair until English Heritage gained Grade 1 Listed Building status for it. At the time of writing it is almost completely restored, thanks to the use of its estate for several high value executive houses.

Relaxing in front of Cound Hall in 1942

We had a spirit stove up in the top floor room, which was strictly taboo, but despite that we occasionally had a bit of a fry-up there. One evening we'd had a really good one - and you know how bacon reeks, a lovely smell - and the Duty Officer came round.... Everything went under the bed pronto, the stove into the cupboard and plates under the bed and we all lit up our fags to kill the smell. Anyway, she came in and she just spoke to us a bit..... She was alright really, was Miss Caley - she was an officer and from a big family, known for Caley's Chocolates.

(Now owned by Nestle, retailing under the 'Caley's Candy' brand.)

But as she was going out she turned and put her head back round and sniffed and said *"There's a very appetising smell in here...."* - she knew darned well what we'd been doing of course, but she didn't seem to bother. She was friendly – too friendly to be a real officer I suppose. I think she'd have preferred to be one of us so that she could relax a bit at times, and enjoy a drink or two - preferably in the company of young men, I'm sure.

I liked it at Cound Hall and we must have been there for about four years - but most of the town girls, as you can imagine, moaned like the very devil - they didn't want to be stuck out in the middle of nowhere. Some of the girls got to like it, it grew on them after a bit, except for the out-and-out townies of course - they didn't like it at all, right to the end.

Jo and Madge, relaxing on the roof of Cound Hall

Relaxing with a bottle of beer up a tree in the grounds of Cound Hall

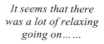

It seems that there was a lot of relaxing going on......

The only recreation was the village pub, The Cound Inn, which this time we were allowed to visit. Same army, but in a different place with different rules. No Redcaps either. Perhaps it was because previously, back in Brecon, we were all very young and they didn't want to have a lot of drunken 18 year olds swanning round the town being a damned nuisance did they? Anyway, at Harlescott they let us use the local pub. But we'd not got an awful lot of money anyway - we were only getting about nine bob a week.

So we used to walk down to the local pub whenever we could and of course we got friendly with all the locals. They were very good to us in the pub there. If we had any food sent to us from home, in the way of bacon or meat or anything, they'd cook it for us. Also when we went away over night we were given ration cards to take with us, for meat and cheese and stuff. Sometimes girls didn't take them and so we used to keep them too. You could always wangle one or two and we used to go and buy some eggs or something and this is when the pub would cook it up for us. They never charged us anything and they'd put vegetables in for us too. And it tasted better than on our illegal spirit stove! Really, people were very kind.

Army Life

When I first got to Harlescott, I was initiated into the do's and don'ts of Army Life very quickly.

I was soon told that the CO was an absolute 'so and so'. I didn't know the woman, I hardly met her, but I was told that she was making their life a misery. About half a dozen of them had got together and written a Letter Of Complaint. Remember, these girls were still all volunteers at this time of the war, early in 1941, and were farmer's daughters and girls from, what shall I say, more well-to-do homes. After all, they could already drive, so they were lucky, intelligent, educated, knew what they were about and able stand up for themselves - or so they thought.

Some of the girls had their own cars and when I arrived there I was horrified because I thought '*Oh crikey - I'm out of my league here!*'

There was a row of cars and I said "*Oh gosh, look at those...are they the Officers' cars?*" and my new friend said "*Oh no, those belong to the drivers*". There was a Lagonda and a Bentley - most of them were expensive sports cars and I really thought '*Oh no - what have I got into now?*'.

But no, they were a great crowd and made us very welcome. The three of us were the first new recruits they'd had and they were really pleased to see us. There was not one of them that I could say was 'snooty' or 'snobbish' in any way. They took us into their arms really and educated us in the wrinkles and what to do and what not to do. What you could get away with and what you couldn't - and they were great. Very loyal to each other and great fun, we laughed most of the time.

There's always an exception, of course. There was one girl, not the brightest of the bunch, but certainly not the poorest either, who had a very nice sports car – I don't know what it was now – and of course she needed petrol for it, but by that time we were on rations for almost everything, including petrol. So, when the coast was clear, she used to go to a chap she knew on the pumps in the lorry bay and slip him a ten bob note to fill her car's tank up. Well, we knew about what she was doing, but it was nothing to do with us – and certainly not me because I didn't have a car!

And then, one day she went there and her pal was off, and someone else was in his place. As I said, she wasn't the brightest of the crowd, so she just tried it on with the new chap.

It served her right – he shopped her. Her pal got it in the neck too, when he got back, but she got a Dishonourable Discharge – not that it would have bothered her, she'd just have gone back to Civvy Street I expect.

Anyway, they'd written this 'Letter of Complaint' to HQ and when I got there, an Enquiry was already going on…. Thank goodness I wasn't mixed up in it, because I might well have been. Anyway, they won the day and the CO was moved - and so were they.

The ringleader, who lived down in Devon, was posted to the north of Scotland. I can't remember the exact places, but this was the sort of thing that happened - if you lived down in the South you were sent up to Scotland and if you lived in Scotland you were sent down to Devon or somewhere far away from home.

The army – you never tried to buck the army because they'd always got you, really.

Drivers and their Lorries

Harlescott, which is where we were, was a VRD – Vehicle Reserve Depot – and we were in Sections A,B,C,D or E. I was in Section C, which was lucky really because it was a good section. There was a sergeant, a corporal and a lance-corporal and then the rest of us. The sections worked together – with two sections if there was a big trip going out, so they'd send A & B, or C & D, or whatever.

The sergeant of my section was a girl called Tid, she was nicknamed Tiddly because she often was tiddly…… Her great friend was Langford Brook, whom we called LB, and she was the sergeant of D Section. If we went on a joint trip it was pretty hilarious to get those two together. We even went to Langford Brook's home once! About half a dozen of us were taking some trucks somewhere and she had wangled to be with us, so she could visit home. Her mother made us very welcome and it was a beautiful place, a great big country house, with stables and dogs and horses. They were great people.

We used to go down to Birmingham, to the factories there, and pick up trucks. We also used to go all the way down to Dagenham and pick up big Fords. You'd be driving something different every day and sometimes the gear-changes were 1,2,3,4,R in an 'H' from top-left to bottom-right, and sometimes they were the other way round: R,3,1,4,2.

We had a girl who came later and she was called Glenys. We used to call her Glenys the Menace and we often wondered how she ever became a driver, but this was later on and they were getting rather desperate for drivers by then….

One time, we were picking up a convoy of mixed Morris and Guy lorries. The Morris' gearbox went 1,2,3,4 and the Guy's was 3,1,4,2, so we were trying to impress on Glenys that if she got a Guy, which was not usual as they were more rare, that the gear box would be the <u>other way round</u>. Anyway we set off and I was in the Maintenance Gang, which meant you travelled at the back, and I could see this truck starting off, and lurching, and stopping. The others overtook it and eventually I caught it up, pulled in front, stopped and went back - and it was Glenys. I said *"What's the matter?"* and she said *"It keeps stalling"*. So I said *"Oh take mine and I'll have a look at it and see if I can find out what's the matter with it."* So I got in it and drove it and off it went perfectly. She'd got it into her head that she'd got a Guy, but she'd got a Morris, so she'd been starting in top and, if she actually got it going, then changing down to first…. This was just the sort of thing Glenys did. It could only have been Glenys.

13

Tanks for the Memory

But most of us, apart from Glenys, had an interesting time because we also used to drive tanks - big tanks too. Churchills, some of them were, or Cromwells, and we used to drive them over to put them onto the train. And of course we enjoyed that.

We used to drive them all the way up from Harlescott Depot to the goods yard, and they'd built a ramp and so then we could to put them straight onto the railway waggons.

We also drove bren-gun carriers and something called a Dragon which was a bit bigger than a bren, steered by two levers, just like a tank. With the bren-gun carrier though, you sat very upright and the wheel was small and right in front of you, horizontal, and once you got going you really had to hang on.... No training for any of this, mind – just get in and find out! So they were interesting.

Each section had a week on Depot Duty, where we did all this sort of thing: loading trains and getting trucks ready for convoys that were going out the next day. So for that week I was 'at home' and it was easier and a bit of a break. Then we'd be off, in and out, for about 6 weeks and then there'd be another week in.

I looked forward to Depot Duty when we used to drive the tanks and load them onto the train. I'd have another driver up in front of me on the waggon, who could see ahead and around, signalling me which way to go. Getting those gigantic tanks onto the train was tricky of course, because I couldn't see much from inside - I'd be going forwards and my 'driver' would just make small gestures with her hand and that was enough to do it. We never had one off though. Lucky, probably.

It was the same when we were parking the trucks, packed in very close together, 'feathered' we called it. Again, we'd have a 'driver' out in front of you shouting *"Left!"* or *"Right!"* or whatever - and woe betide you if you looked round because you'd get cussed by somebody or other because they could see where you were going and you couldn't....

But that June it was very hot I remember and we were just in drill trousers and a shirt and a pair of pants and a bra and we were wringing wet. I used to think to myself *"Not as bad as those poor devils in the desert...."* - you know, inside those tanks, all day long in the desert heat - I don't know how they survived. Everything you touched was hot, the metal was the worst, you could have fried an egg on it. It was just a bit uncomfortable at times.

We also used to drive scout cars sometimes, which had a little slit to look through which was only about two inches deep and about six inches wide. So you always had to have a lookout with you in the thing. She would stand up, out of the hatch, and could see what was going on, around round-abouts and guide us safely across junctions.

The Daimler Scout Car

14

But to get in it you had to lift open the square, steel hatch in the top and lower yourself down. Well, being tall I had a bit of a job getting in because they weren't very roomy. I had to hang on to the lip with my hands up above me and wriggle my body down into the seat.

I was doing this one day when the lid fell shut, down onto my fingers and anchored me there. So I was yelling blue murder for somebody to come and rescue me. My lookout had gone to the loo or something I expect, but she wasn't with me anyway. In time, the others came running over and got me out - and I'd got eight bleeding fingers. They took me in the loo and we'd always got some First Aid kit somewhere I suppose and they bandaged me up. I had the marks to show for it for quite a long time afterwards.

We also had to drive Quads*, a big, covered-in thing that was freezing cold in winter and boiling hot in summer – we hated them!

Morris C8 Quad

* **Quad** Officially referred to as the Morris Commercial C8 FAT (Field Artillery Tractor), but commonly known as the 'Quad', this was an artillery tractor used by the British and Commonwealth forces throughout World War II.
Fulfilling requirements including being four-wheel drive and capable of chemical defence, although not being armoured it replaced the earlier Light Dragon and was used to tow field artillery pieces such as the 25 pounder gun-howitzer and anti-tank guns such as the 17 pounder.

Chapter 3
NEW EXPERIENCES

Convoys

A ll the vehicles were parked at the VRDs, Vehicle Reserve Depots that is, and that's where we'd collect the trucks from to take them to the docks, or wherever. But also we'd bring older trucks back to there sometimes, and the section on 'Depot Duty' would park them ready for Maintenance to deal with them the next day.

So then they'd go through the Maintenance Bay and there was a permanent gang of maintenance girls who did all this, oil changes and things. What oil they had to put in would depend where they were going eventually: thick oil for the desert and thin oil for Russia.

And then the duty drivers drove them off and parked them properly. If there was a convoy going out the next morning, they'd see that they were all filled up with petrol, oil, water and everything, and lined up ready to go.

The next morning it was over to us, and we'd just get up and in and away we'd go, wherever it was we were going to that day. So it was an interesting life because usually you went somewhere different every day.

We went to all the ports of course: Liverpool, Portsmouth, Swansea, Southampton, and sometimes other ports too. Just backwards and forwards, all over England, Wales and Scotland, all the time.

For the first two years or so, most of the trucks we drove from Harlescott were open. They'd come from the factories which had built them, but usually all the breakable parts, including the windscreens and side-screens, were safely packed away in the back. So for us, there was often no windscreen, no hood, no anything. There was a little postage stamp windscreen sometimes, which didn't help very much. The 15Cwt Bedfords usually had screens, but the canvas tilt (roof) was packed away.

What's more, even in winter we didn't have much in the way of good clothing to keep us warm. Just our uniforms and a long leather army waistcoat, and anything more that our mums could knit for us.

Ackroyd, aka Acky;
Madge;
Jo;
A.N.Other

Incidents

My very first trip was to somewhere north of Nottingham, in the fog, in an American left-hand drive lorry. This was the first lhd vehicle I'd ever driven, so it was in at the deep end for me.

There were incidents, of course. We had one big, quite tough trip to Scotland. We'd set off early in the morning on this particular trip, there were about 30 of us I think, and it was pouring with rain, but we'd only gone about half a mile and my truck boiled. It had run out of water. Well, there were two taps – there was the one on the side of the cylinder block and there was the one at the bottom of the radiator. To get to the radiator tap you had to lie on your back on the road and reach up and turn it on or off. You either got icy cold or boiling hot water up your sleeve. Sometimes someone had neglected to turn one of them on or off correctly and that's what had happened to me. So down on the wet road I had to get and turn this damned tap off.

And then it all needed to be filled up again, so we went to a cottage nearby and got some warm water and poured it in, and back again, and again, until we'd filled it up and could set off once more. We caught the others up at Preese Heath, where they'd stopped for a coffee break at a transport café we used to like. It was still lashing down with rain, but we kept going until we hit Warrington – we were heading for Scotland.

We'd stopped in a cobbled square and all went into a fish & chip café, which had got a restaurant upstairs. We were sitting up there having fish & chips and somebody said *"Hey! Look out of the window!"*. And I've never before or since seen such big snowflakes, they were like saucers! By the time we got out, the snow on my seat was about 6 inches deep. And we were supposed to be going to Carlisle that night....

Anyway, after a lot of getting stuck, and digging out, and sliding, and slithering we eventually got as far as Kendal. So we went to the police station in Kendal - they were used to us coming in out of the blue because we often had to stay over at Kendal, but there were a lot of us that time. We usually stayed in private houses that were on the list, or sometimes in one of the local pubs. The people of Kendal, I have to say, were very good to us. Anyway, as usual they found billets for us, and five others and myself were in the Mason's Arms.

The family in the pub where the six of us were staying were wonderful. They'd got a big sitting room and they lit a great big roaring fire for us. Then the landlady took all our wet outer clothes and said *"I'll get 'em dried for you"* and I know we sat round this fire, wrapped in blankets, while they did us a lovely meal. We sat there talking for quite a while and I must admit we got a little bit tiddly that night. I think it was just because we'd been so darned cold.

Nevertheless, we got up early the next morning and were off. Oh but, as usual, we'd drained the trucks of water before we left them the night before, so in the crisp, cold morning light, it was down and under again, on our backs in the snow, turning the blooming taps off, back out and up, and fill the radiators up again. There was no anti-freeze in those days. After a bit we did learn that, if it was frosty at night, you had to wait till the truck had drained all the warm water out and then get down and turn this tap back off again, because otherwise it would freeze in position and you couldn't move it in the morning. That was later on, but on that occasion we hadn't learned the tip yet and so got down there in the morning and most of the taps were well and truly frozen solid. With kettles of hot water from the house we did get them moved - but then we had to fill the rads of course. We were in quite deep snow by then, but we borrowed some buckets from somewhere and filled the trucks from the river – because all the outside taps were frozen too. We were in the car park, down by the river - I think its still there.

17

At about this point, the police came over and told us how it was.

"You certainly can't get over Shap* today, no chance! We'll have to try and sort you out a different route."

So they lined us all up on the outskirts of Kendal, and there we waited – and waited. I think it was on the Ullswater Road and the dear ladies in the houses came out with jugs of hot drinks and biscuits for us. They were suffering from rationing too of course, but I suppose they felt sorry for us and they were wonderful. We had to run the engines every quarter of an hour to stop them from freezing. The engines that is, not us – the lorries didn't have the luxury of heaters! It was so cold. We were stamping the ground and walking up and down trying to keep warm and so when all these ladies came out with jugs of hot drinks we thought it was wonderful.

"Well.... you might get through or you might not" the policeman finally said. *"So what do you want to do?"*

"We'll have a go". It was a matter of honour for us that we got to the docks to catch the boat, because if the boat missed the convoy and tried going on its own it was likely to end up going down to the bottom of the deep blue sea. The convoy would come round to 3 or 4 ports, picking more up at each stage - they didn't all start from the same docks – but they couldn't wait for just one to get loaded.

So for us it was just a day to get going.... and get stuck, dig out, get going, get stuck, dig out ......all day.

At one stage we came to a little village on the A6 just north of Kendal - I've no idea what it was called but it had a very steep bank going down to it and another even longer one up out of it. We had to be careful going down it on the packed snow – there was a farmhouse on the left at the bottom – but it was even worse getting back up out of it. We had an awful job getting up this bank and I was the last one to manage it. At the top I drew on a bit, stopped, and walked back to see if anyone else was coming. I was a bit doubtful, because I'd had such an awful job – I'd needed about three shots at it before I'd made it, packing the snow into ice, and they just couldn't follow me. There were about six of them behind me. We called to each other but, because they just couldn't get through at all, they went back to Kendal. They were stuck there for about four days.

It was still snowing on and off and the snow was deep - you don't ever see snow like it down here in Worcestershire.

* **Shap**   At Shap summit, on the A6 is about 1350 feet above sea level; there is now a memorial to such drivers and crews as Jo and her pals.

Until 1970, and the completion of the M6 between Kendal and Penrith, the A6 across Shap summit formed the main north-south route, linking the industrial areas of northwest England with Scotland. The route was busy and notoriously hazardous in poor weather conditions. Often in winter the road became snow-bound and impassable. Ironically, when the M6 arrived, it spelt disaster to many businesses on which the economy of the village relied.

THIS MEMORIAL PAYS TRIBUTE TO THE DRIVERS AND CREWS OF VEHICLES THAT MADE POSSIBLE THE SOCIAL AND COMMERCIAL LINKS BETWEEN NORTH AND SOUTH ON THIS OLD AND DIFFICULT ROUTE OVER SHAP FELL BEFORE THE OPENING OF THE M6 MOTORWAY.
REMEMBERED TOO ARE THOSE WHO BUILT AND MAINTAINED THE ROAD AND THE GENERATIONS OF LOCAL PEOPLE WHO GAVE FREELY OF FOOD AND SHELTER TO STRANDED TRAVELLERS IN BAD WEATHER.

Anyway, off I went then, tearing after the others, who were way ahead of me by then. You were always supposed to, under all conditions, look out for the one behind you. If the one behind you stopped, you'd stop, because if you got stuck, especially up there, all on your own, well - I don't know – you'd die I think.

You feel very puny up there and think '*My God, old Mother Nature can squash you like a fly if she wants to.....*' There's all these vast areas of open space and all this snow, and nobody around for miles and miles. We didn't have mobile 'phones in those days, y'know! You'd think - what would you do if you conked out and you were on your own - you wouldn't have a hope. Not in an open truck you wouldn't.

Anyway the girl who was in front of me had forgotten all about this and had gone on, keeping up with her pals. So there I was, high up in the Fells and heading north in a big, open truck, all on my own, and going like a bat out of hell along empty, snow-packed roads....

I wouldn't do it now, but then I was young and daft and all I thought about was catching the others up.

I came to the top of a bank and the narrow road dipped down steeply, with stone walls on either side and a narrow grass verge just showing through the edge of the snow. Right at the top of the bank there was a big artic that was in the process of just starting to jack-knife. I thought '*Hells bells - he's going to block the road!*'. So I put my foot down and flew down this bank and up the other side - and <u>just</u> got through between this truck and the wall. I stopped at the top, looked back and there he was, wedged. I shouted to them that I'd tell somebody and then kept going - and came round the corner and there was my convoy. They weren't waiting for me, oh no, they were just having a break, stamping around, ready to head off for the last leg to Carlisle. I can't quite remember, but I might have told 'em what I thought......

Since breakfast in Kendal, we hadn't had a meal all day. Where we'd stopped along the way, usually they couldn't give us their food. We did get hot drinks and some biscuits, but because of the snow the local people didn't know how long they'd be cut off - and they couldn't stock up like they could in peacetime, because of the rationing. They didn't know how long this snow was going to last, but they did their best, although we didn't have a meal as such.

I think, if I remember correctly, it's only about 45 to 50 miles from Kendal to Carlisle, but the first ones didn't get to Carlisle before five o'clock. I left Kendal at about eleven in the morning and got there about ten o'clock at night. Frozen.

When we got there, I can remember going round and round the camp at Carlisle to try to get some hot water to wash and fill a hot-water-bottle. Carlisle Camp was an awful place and we all hated it. It was called Hadrian's Camp and we used to wish Hadrian had camped somewhere else....

The next morning we got up, filled up and set off for Glasgow. It was a repeat of the day before really - and then we came to a giant snowdrift. We all dug and we got through it and kept going into the dark evening. It was just very, very slow.

We'd got to the top of some hills; I don't think we were that far from Glasgow by then. It was about ten o'clock at night I should think, when we came across a Queen Mary stuck across the road, with a fearsome drop on one side......

A Queen Mary was a long 60 foot low-loader trailer with a tractor-unit up front and it was used to transport aeroplane parts
– a long, giant outfit, hence the name.

A Queen Mary moving the fuselage of a Short Sunderland flying-boat.

Of course, we couldn't get past him, so we all had to stop and try to help. As well as the driver, there was an RAF officer with this Queen Mary and by then there were about 20 of us, but it still looked quite hopeless. However, this officer had a bottle of rum and he passed that round, we all had a swig, and he organised us. Amazingly enough, before too long, between us we managed to push it off and out of the way!

Mind you, having got that monster out of the way, we still couldn't get away. We were about to set off, but there towards the back was one of our drivers, just sat in the truck, not moving. She was just sat in her seat, not doing anything. Looking back now, I'm sure she was suffering from hyper-thermia, but you'd never heard of that in those days - you were just 'darned cold'.

We didn't know what to do - we hadn't a clue - we just followed our instincts. We got her down out of her truck, lifted her out really, and kept her moving. Swinging her arms about, we were working her arms up and down with us marching her up and down in the snow. It was deep, but it had got a bit packed down and so we walked her up and down as well as we could. You can imagine what it was like, struggling with her through the deep snow. Then the RAF officer gave her a swig of his rum and she came to. We got her talking and moving for herself and she got there all right in the end.

I think it was just before midnight we were doing all this, it was certainly well after midnight when the last of us got to Glasgow. The RTOs – Railway Transport Officers – took us in a lorry to the hotel where we were staying in Souchiehall Street. However, in hotels in those days after about 8 o'clock at night you'd got no hope of getting anything except a drink at the bar – and by the time we got there even the bars were shut! But they'd got a big fire in the lounge, so we all crowded around it. There were about seven or eight of us there, being the last to arrive, the others already having gone to bed.

So we sat by this fire, feeling hungry and very sorry for ourselves, all bedraggled, dirty and absolutely wacked. However there were some Canadian RAF boys staying there too, and they came in soon after we'd settled down.

"Hey babes, who are you then? Where've you come from? You OK?" We briefly told them, and said that we were so hungry.... And they said *"Well you gotta to have a meal or something.....?"* We told them there was no chance at that time of night, but they just smiled.

"Leave it to us….." they said - and vanished.

So there we were, sitting by the fire, trying to thaw out, and in my head I can still see the doors opening and those boys coming through. They'd got a giant plate of thick sandwiches. I think they'd cut them themselves. I reckon they'd raided the hotel's kitchens and also got two big pots of coffee and a bottle - I don't know if it was scotch or rum – but it was so very welcome! Anyway, they sat down and we all tucked into this lot together. It turned into a lovely evening after an awful day. Those boys really saved our bacon. We went to bed and slept very well indeed.

But then we had to put all our wet clothes on again the next morning ready to go back home by train.

So, all round, that was some trip.

There was a follow-up though. Apparently, while we were away the Queen, who later became the Queen Mum, had come to Harlescote to see what we were up to. They told her about our trip to Glasgow and what we'd been through......

And then, about a week after, she talked about it all on the wireless!

My mother heard it and she said to my father "*I hope Joan wasn't on that trip!*" But of course I was - and it was quite an experience!

London and Flying Bombs

We used to go down to London a lot and it was pretty horrific. I was in London later on when the flying-bombs came over. I was on my own at the time, delivering a staff car to some unit in London. A policeman jumped out and stopped me and shouted at us.

"*Get out! Get out! There's a doodle-bug!*" Anyway I shot out - you didn't argue in wartime if anyone said '*Get out*' or '*Run*' or '*Duck*' - you just did it quick. I think we lay down by the car and this thing landed about half a mile away up the road, but it wouldn't have been very good if I'd kept going - I'd have ended up a bit nearer than I would have wanted to be.

I was also in London when the first V2 fell, but we didn't know what it was because there was no warning like a doodle-bug or a bomb. You could hear the bombs whistling down and you could hear the strange noise of the doodle-bugs, until they suddenly stopped – and then it was time to take cover. But with the V2 there was just this great crash. They travelled faster than sound, I was told.

In London we were billeted in a big apartment block, which was for the staff of Selfridges before the war. It was all little rooms and bathrooms dotted about here and there. Of course, all the billets used for transit were on top floors, while the others for the permanent London staff that were working in the War Office and places like that, were the lower rooms. Every time I stopped over in London, there was bit more glass broken and a bit more plaster missing in the top floors. Soon all the windows were boarded up anyway. This particular night when one of those things went off, I was washing and I jerked up and banged my head on the washbasin shelf. The plaster flew, the door burst open, stuff fell off and hit the floor – but we were used to this sort of thing happening - it was normal we thought – just a rather big one this time. So we tidied up, sorted things out and went downstairs and out to get a meal somewhere, but there was a great fuss in the streets - nobody seemed to know quite what it was. It was the first V2.

Of course both the V1s and V2s came down quite often after that for a while. We were going to London during the Blitz and afterwards on an average of once a week, I should think, and we'd have to stay overnight, and I can't honestly say that I was frightened. We were young and none of us thought we could ever get killed. It happened to other people, it didn't happen to us. I think that's what keeps you going really, because you don't imagine... That's why we get heroes I suppose. Now of course, I'd be petrified I expect! I should know damn well it <u>could</u> happen to me.

Another time we arrived to find London in one its infamous smogs. That was a bad fog loaded with smoke from all the coal that was being burned to keep warm in winter. They don't get smogs in London any more, thank goodness, because of all the rules about not using anything other than smoke-free fuels. Anyway, when we got there we just couldn't see ahead of us and so the Police took us through. In fact, they often did that anyway and so it was planned well ahead that we should meet up with a police patrol that would take us directly to our destination. How the hell they got a convoy of trucks right through London, in a thick smog, arriving at the right place, without losing any of us, I really don't know.....

But, coming back the next day by train from Paddington, we were taking a towrope back with us. It took two of us to carry the big, oily, heavy lump, but we were doing all right - until we got to the platform. We all had rail passes of course, so we were sent straight through, but the guard told us to get a move on as the train was about to leave. We made it, in a bit of a rush, just as the train began to move. I was at the back, as usual, and my pal held the coach door open for me. At that point I slipped up the step and went down with a thump on top of this heavy towrope. I can remember lying there, flat out, a bit surprised and a little hurt, and looking up. All I could see were slim, very expensive ladies shoes, with elegant silk stockinged legs in them..... We'd landed in a coach full of a dozen or more glamorous, well made-up young ladies, maybe chorus girls or the cast from a West End show, or something - but we certainly didn't fit in! We all thought it was very funny. They didn't, though.

I was in some quite bad raids in London, but I never went down in the shelters because, for me, that was the worst horror of all. I'm claustrophobic and I can't stand being shut in.

The people used to sleep down in the Tube too, in the Underground, and for me that would have been hell. There was one woman in particular that, by the end of the war, really should have had a medal. There were all these people, poor devils, lying there sleeping, kids and all because some of them hadn't been evacuated to the country. None of them knew whether they were going to have a home to go back to in the morning, whether it had gone up in smoke or been knocked flat. Sometimes they used to get a bit low of course and this woman - she was what you'd imagine a typical Cockney to be - a big, hefty woman she was, would have them up on their feet, dancing up and down the platform. You know, '*Roll Out The Barrel*' and all that sort of thing. Night after night. I used to think '*What a woman!*'

A different memory I have from during the time of the Blitz is one sunny Sunday when we were going up through the Lake District. I had been right in the middle of London just a few days before, but there in the Lakes we were surrounded by blossom on the trees and it was just a perfect May morning, deep in the countryside. It was quiet and, even driving an open truck, when we went by we could hear the birds singing - I can clearly remember that morning.

I found it hard to believe the horror of what was going on elsewhere, not so very far away really, it just didn't seem possible...... It was like another world.....

Girl Drivers?

We drivers did have a bit of a hard time at times, but we did it and we surprised people with what we did.

So I can't honestly say that we were miserable. There was always somebody who could see the funny side of everything. There always is in a gang of people I suppose, when you're all together, you're all good mates and there's always somebody to help you. You're not on your own at all really. Oh, we had one or two hard trips, but we had some good trips as well, particularly in the summer. In those open trucks in summer it was lovely and I thoroughly enjoyed it.

There's a lovely pub in Shrewsbury called The Boathouse on New Street, overlooking the River Severn, below The Quarry. We used to stop there and they used to cook a fry-up, just for us. They were really very good to us women drivers and I'm afraid that eventually, maybe inevitably, we became a bit elitist.... Almost everywhere we went we were feted, wined and dined because people had never seen girls driving lorries before. They'd never seen girls driving at all in most cases.

I also remember being in Wales, at the bottom of the Horseshoe Pass out of Llangollen, where there's a terrific bend at the bottom. There were some women standing and admiring us, asking us who we were and where were from and what we were doing.

"You girls are never driving these big trucks?" they said, and then along comes an old boy who insisted on giving us innocent, inexperienced girls his good advice.

"If you miss your gears at the bottom of that hill you'll be down here backwards before you can breathe." But we'd heard all about this hill before and so I made sure I'd got it down into bottom gear before I got to this bend..... So we all got to the top, although it did take us about quarter of an hour to do it. I was a bit miffed that the old boy wasn't up there to see us!

Another time we took some trucks up to Stranraer on Loch Ryan, on the Southwest coast of Scotland. It's used as a ferry port to Belfast now, but then there were transports waiting for our trucks. Anyway, when we got there they couldn't billet us in Stranraer, they were all full up. So they took us due West to a little village called Portpatrick, right out on the coast. Well, I don't think they'd ever seen a girl in uniform before and they made a terrific fuss of us! There was a dance going on in the village hall that evening and we were invited to go. We didn't need asking twice, I can tell you.

One of the girls who was with us was called Mitch and she had Eton style cropped hair and was very hefty and really, she did look a bit like a chap.... Don't forget that we were all in uniform and that was a shirt, tie, blouson jacket and trousers. Not the best outfit for girls to go to the dance in! But, there we were and there was a 'Ladies Excuse Me' dance and one of the local girls came up and 'excused' Mitch. Mitch came from Devon and wasn't shy...

"Oh, yes, that's all right m'dear, come on" and she grabbed this girl and they went waltzing off around the hall. Of course, the local girl soon realised and was covered in embarrassment in front of all her friends watching from the side. We were killing ourselves laughing too - we thought it was the funniest thing out. Poor girl!

Everyday Dangers

I suppose my worst experience was going right by an unexploded bomb. I can't remember where it was, but we'd got to get to the docks and there was only one way to get there. They'd suffered from a lot of air raids and many of the roads were blown up.

The Bomb Disposal people were there and the officer said *"Well, if you've got to go through, I suppose you've got to – but for God's sake you be careful!"* They pointed it out to us and I could see it down the road, sticking up out of the footpath. So they gave us a lecture and said *"Now you go very, very slowly, in bottom gear, one at a time. Be sure, mind, don't you go rushin' through or we'll be havin' to sweep you up later....."* So we went as far over to the other side as we could and crawled along in bottom gear. I was on Maintenance Duty again, waiting at the back, and I thought *'By the time I get there they'll have upset the damned thing, just ready and waiting for me....'* As it turned out, I had to laugh at how the Police looked, hiding behind the sandbags while I was chatting with the B-D lads as our first lorries were going by. Anyway we survived, we all got past.

Looking back it's quite amusing, but I don't know that it really was at the time.

What wasn't quite so amusing was when I had the brakes give out on a big truck with a trailer, going down Rownham Hill, below Clifton suspension bridge, en route to the docks in Bristol. I kept it in gear though and eventually came to a stop. That was a bit hairy too.

When we were on Depot Duty, we were sometimes able to go to dances in Shrewsbury. They had them at Morris' Café, which was downstairs, and that could be quite exciting sometimes, especially when the Americans came to Shrewsbury. Sometimes there'd be a fight, as there often was with the Americans. I remember one night, one of the black Yanks had got up and asked a white girl for a dance and she'd said OK. Well, of course the white Americans objected to this - they were very racist and so there was a fight. In two minutes there was all hell going on. Very soon, at each corner of the stairs which came down from the café, there was an American MP - with a tommy gun. We all dived under the tables, thinking *'What if they start spraying those things about?'* They didn't of course - they just took those that were scrapping away, both blacks and whites, and locked them all up. I'm sure they must have killed some of them on the way, because they used to just hit them on the head and sling them in the back of the jeep..... Then they roared away, they had no sympathy for them, believe you me. They were pretty tough. And then the dance got going again as if nothing had happened.

Then I had one experience which was really very unpleasant. We were on Depot Duty again, and a girl was coming down from the depot with a pick-up and for some reason it caught fire underneath. I think in those days they had a habit of spraying old oil over everything that might rust and then I think it had got muck, dirt and dust on it as well. If there was a petrol leak too, it just took a spark from a brake or something and it would go up, and not go out with all that oily muck going too. I grabbed a Pyrene - a fire extinguisher - out of one of the trucks and lay down on the ground, pumping it up at the flames underneath. And then the idiot that had been driving it had got out - and started pumping another Pyrene across underneath and right into my face! I got the fire out, but I'd got some of the stuff in my eyes. I really thought I was blind! That did frighten me. Fortunately, our sergeant had just driven up in a pick-up and she whipped me off down to Shrewsbury Hospital. It was awful being taken in, you know, *"Up two steps, come along, turn right, turn left...."* I couldn't see a thing and it was very, very painful. But they were wonderful at the hospital - they irrigated my eyes and then they got a doctor to get them dressed and he gave me a painkiller. I was off duty for about a week after that and I had to go down to the hospital every day to have my eyes washed out. Touch wood, they're still OK.

Only three weeks after that, we were towing some old vehicles away for scrapping. Just towards the end of the war, REME used to get as many old vehicles going again as they could, and then they'd put the others on tow. This was to take them to Ministry of Supply Depots where they were scrapped. I was being towed in something, I don't know what it was, but this thing had got no foot brake, just a vestige of a hand brake. We were coming from Shrewsbury and going down towards Wenlock Edge before you climb up that long climb, heading East. Well, this thing set on fire - and there were flames coming right up through the floorboards! This thing was a left-hand drive and I was being towed by a right-hand drive. I couldn't make her see by waving my arms about because she had no mirrors or anything like that in front, and I had no horn. So I thought *'What the hell am I going to do?'* Now, I'd towed with this girl before, so I thought the only thing to do is to let the hand brake go and hope it would over-run the tow rope, bump into her and she'd stop. Which it did and fortunately she stopped - but by this time I was already out on the running board, and then off and running! I didn't want to get burned and I certainly didn't want another taste of a Pyrene fire extinguisher! So the minute I smelt it, I was off up the road - I thought the damned thing could burn as far as I was concerned!

They got the fire out and pushed the thing off into a field and we carried on, with me as a passenger in a slightly safer lorry.

War's End

Towards the end of the war I had to do three months on driving instruction, which I didn't enjoy very much. Well, you had no dual control vehicles as you have nowadays, there was the person you were teaching sitting at the controls and you sitting by the side. All you could do was grab the hand-brake…. and some of the trainees were hopeless!

It was when they were conscripted, and not volunteers like us, that's when we had a different sort of girl coming in. There were girls from all backgrounds by then, but a really good mix, which is what you needed I suppose. I mean they were still a good crowd, but they weren't all perfect by any means. It didn't bother me – you gravitate towards your own sort of course, people with your own interests, your own standards and your own background to a certain extent. It's inevitable because you've got more in common.

So there were girls from all walks of life, but as I said, in the beginning they were mostly from well-to-do homes because they were the only girls who could drive early on. However, when things got tougher in the war and they started getting short of drivers, they did start teaching all sorts of people to drive. And like I said, some of them were really useless, although most were very good and an asset to our Unit.

After the war, Joan and I used to compare our experiences with the 'townies'. She'd had to try to turn Birmingham girls into useful Land Army workers in just four weeks.

"Poor little devils," she told me, *"they didn't know what had hit them! Probably never seen anything more animated than a bus before and said they'd never seen the sun so bright! But some of them just couldn't take it and ran off home."*

For me it was the ack-ack girls that I'd have to try to teach to drive – but they were in the Army and couldn't run off! We did laugh!

But, with your own sort, you build up a companionship that you never ever get again anywhere else, however good friends you are.

I think in the army it's a special relationship because you rely on each other so much. It's all you've got: each other. Especially in our job, where we were away on our own for so much of the time. There was usually no officer to go running to if you were in trouble - all you'd got were your pals.

So you did look after each other. You were like a big family and you made your own little group of friends inside it.

Demobilisation

I was demobbed from Shrewsbury in '46, so I must have been there for about five years. I enjoyed every minute of it, the army life and the people I met. The local people for example - we got quite friendly with a lot of them. Mostly farmers and they were good to us. They'd invite you there to tea and that sort of thing, and help us out on the road, as I've told earlier.

I very nearly volunteered to stay on, because by that time I loved the army, but my father was ill and so I had to come home.

Chapter 4

A RESTART

Back in Civvy Street

In 1946, when I'd been discharged from the army, my father had a heart attack and so I had to go straight home. I lived there, in Cedar Cottage on the Rydd, for a time and then my father got a bit better - but by then he'd got angina, so I stayed around.

Frank & Marge Knighton, who was the Chief Accountant at Cadburys, and Tom Newell's (centre) best friend.

Living at home was fine, but I nevertheless had to get a job pronto because I had no money, only about £100 which was what I'd come out of the army with. So I went to work for a chap called Basil Moss, over by the Three Counties Showground, who was a pig and poultry farmer. I didn't like pigs and poultry very much though - I really wanted to get back with horses.

I did have a little mongrel dog for a time, a funny little thing that kept running away. The last time it did that, it ended up in Leigh Sinton and so I told the people who had it that they could keep it. That saved my father all the trouble of repeatedly having to go to collect it from wherever it was that time.

So I then went to work for a friend of my parents called Bill Yardley later in 1946. His wife was lovely, but he and I didn't really see eye to eye - I didn't like the way he treated his animals.

It was at about this time that I first met Joan Bradshaw. Then later, while I was exercising Yardley's horses one day, I met up with Joan again, who was also exercising horses from the next farm, Woodsfield. So Joan and I decided it was just as well to exercise the horses together. More fun for them and for us too.

Joan clearly remembered that first meeting too, but in a little more detail:

"I suppose it was a small but significant contretemps really. I was riding my horse, Robin, along the Guarlford Straight, going home, when we were startled by being passed by a motorbike - at speed. When I'd calmed Robin down, I caught up and the bike had stopped around the bend, looking back. I told the rider just what I thought of it! Well, the rider turned out to be Joan Newell, and she was a girl of much my own age and, well, you might think it was silly, but we became friends." *

Anyway, that's what we did and eventually I left Yardley and went to work for Harold Tolley alongside Joan. It was Gaffer Tolley, as everybody always called him – even his own kids - who was so very helpful when we started farming, which I will come to later.

Riding

So we had quite a good life with the Gaffer. Joan looked after the horses mainly and I helped with the other stock. I used to fodder the cattle and that sort of thing, and then we'd both exercise the horses. So we were paid for spending two hours per day riding and getting horses fit for hunting and then, when the hunting season started, we had at least one day's hunting a week as well!

Then we'd go Point-to-Pointing after Christmas, which was great fun, and we'd be getting paid for all this, mind. I drove the lorry. We went down to Larkhill, Newbury, and all over the place with the horses, and to all the local courses.

The old man's hunter was called Donegal, or Donny for short, which Joan showed in the Hunter Class at the local shows. He often won, so we thoroughly enjoyed that too. He also had a mare called Carlisle Bay, and I exercised her and I rode her for hunting too, but she was a bit of a clumsy bugger because she fell with me out hunting once, out on the flat, but we were going at a fair lick so I was thrown clear. I did break my collarbone though.

Jo on Conker & Joan on Jimmy in Chipping Campden in 1949

* Friends. Despite a seemingly inauspicious start, they were indeed close friends and partners for the next sixty years. To distinguish between *'The Two Joans'*, Miss Newell was thereafter usually called *'Jo'* by Mr.& Mrs. Bradshaw and others, or *'Big Joan'* by some of the locals.

Then Joan rode her at a Point-to-Point at Bushley, where she fell at the first fence and dislocated Joan's shoulder.

We then took her to Alcester Point-to-Point, where she was ridden by Ted Bomford. She fell again. Tragically, Ted was kicked in the head by another passing horse, and was killed.

While she would have been perfect for flat racing, that's not what the Gaffer did of course, so her next outing was at Lark Hill with Tony May on top. Yet again she fell, but this time she broke her back. She did of course have to be put down on the spot. Some people did say *"Bloody good job too!"* but they didn't really mean it. She was a lovely bay mare and could have done dressage as she moved beautifully, but she just couldn't cope with rough ground. It wasn't very good going back to Woodsfield with an empty lorry. (The Gaffer was sick in bed and didn't know anything about this of course.)

When we got half way back, through Malborough, a friend of ours called Frank Mason was jumping up and down in front of the Castle & Ball, so we stopped and he took us into the pub where he'd arranged a big plate of sandwiches and a few scotches for us.

The worst thing of all is coming down in the morning to an empty stable, with no head looking for you over the door..... It hits you hard just then – and really hurts.

While getting the point-to-pointers fit, we used to go to Holland Martin Gallops on Breedon Hill. This was great fun for us.

Occasionally, Freddie Rimell would let us use his gallops at Kinnersley. He was the trainer and he had some super gallops there. He was a very nice chap was Fred and he didn't mind you going. His wife, Mercy Rimell, was a bit of a dragon really, but she had to put up with us and we got on alright. One time while we were waiting to go up with the second string, half a dozen of his lads, mounted on very valuable racehorses, spent the time jumping a fallen tree trunk. We thought that had Mercy, who had gone up with the first string, come back and caught them at this stupid trick, she'd have killed 'em. Joan and I were naturally worried about the horses, but it was none of our business - but Mercy would have had <u>no</u> mercy!

What's more, after the racing at Worcester Racecourse had finished, they'd let us school our horses there, which was really good. At this time Carlisle Bay was fit and the old man told me to try her out and see what she could do. There were about six of us and at the bottom bend I just squeezed and asked the mare – and she took off like a bullet, which was the most fantastic feeling in the world.

The other Point-to-Pointer we had at the time was Robin Adair. Joan had Robin when he was four, when he was hunted lightly and by the time he was five and six he was hunted hard, which taught him to look after himself. He was Point-to-Pointed for seven years. He never fell and I think I'm right in saying that he was rarely out of the first three in any event. His safety record was due, I believe, to the fact that he was hunted fairly hard in his youth.

You have to hunt the horses eight times to get them qualified to run in the Point-to-Point. Then you had to get your card signed by the Master when you'd done your three hours, and you had really to be seen to be hunting properly, no hanging about at the back, mind.

Whenever we took the horses racing, Frank Doorbar, a neighbouring farmer, always came with Joan and me in the lorry. He was good fun and we used to laugh all the way there and back.

One interesting episode I recall was while I was working for Gaffer Tolley was when I was exercising one of the point-to-pointers and I came up over Balls Hill, which is off the Gloucester Drive going towards Upper Woodsfield. It's on a hill overlooking Madresfield, which we called 'The Parks'. Just then my horse suddenly stopped dead and his ears pricked forward and he was looking across towards the Gloucester Drive - and then I heard a hunting horn. Obviously he'd heard them before me, but I heard hounds too and across The Parks came a fox. It got to the brook, went in it and up it about, I don't know, 30 or 40 yards, which lost its scent, then it came out of the brook and trotted up the bank and sat down, looking back. I couldn't believe it, about 6 feet away from my horse! Of course it wouldn't smell me downwind and up on the horse, and it just sat there looking at what was going on. It was very interested and you could see its head move as it was following the path of the hounds across the Gloucester Drive, or The Parks as it's also called. The hounds worked up and down the brook until one of them picked up the fox's line, as he'd come out of the water. At this, the fox just stood up, stretched a hind leg out like a dog does, and just loped off.

It was extraordinary.

Tractors

As I said, I used to fodder Gaffer Tolley's cattle, and I used a tractor and trailer. I drove his Fordson Major, which was a big tall tractor - a bit top heavy I always thought. Anyway, I used to pull the trailer over to the Gloucester Drive, with hay for the cattle that were turned out there. Harold Tolley's son, Christopher, who was about four or five at the time, used to come running after me. He followed me about like a puppy dog for some reason and he used to want to come foddering the cattle with me, which meant he had to sit in the trailer. Of course that's not allowed nowadays, but I used to sit him in the corner of the trailer and I used to wag my finger at him and say *"Don't you dare move,"* because I used to think that if anything happened to Christopher I'd have to emigrate. But he was very, very good and he did exactly what he was told. I suppose he knew that if he didn't behave he couldn't come again.

Shirley Tolley, Harold's daughter, used to help sometimes and one day we were foddering the cattle and I was on the trailer and Shirley was driving the tractor. I looked up and we were heading straight for the brook! I yelled at her *"Shirley! turn the wheel,"* but she'd frozen, she was going straight for the brook. So I had to jump down off the trailer, you can just imagine this, and run and catch up the tractor, get on the tractor, and get hold of the steering wheel. I can tell you we made it with just a few feet to spare…. How we didn't go in the brook I'll never know. She'd just frozen - it was most strange.

We survived and I think I must have had a charmed life in those days, what with the big horses, tractors and open machinery, all surrounded by children and cattle…..

A Mad Bull

We had an Ayrshire bull there who was as mad as a hatter. We couldn't keep him in and so we'd put what we call a logger on him, which is a length of wood about three foot long with a chain in the middle. That goes over his neck and so the piece of wood hangs against his legs as he walks – that usually slows them down. But then he got stuck in the boozey, which is the passage behind the cowshed, behind the mangers. He got wedged there really firmly and we had an awful job to get him out. We did get him out eventually - and so he ran off and jumped the far gate – a five-barred gate it was! – still with this logger on him!

The old man decided then that he had better go to market. But, while we still had him, he was shut in the yard at the back of the barn, which had a seven-foot high stone wall around it. The old man told me *"Shut the bugger in there until we take him to market - and you can feed him in there and keep him in there!"* So there I was, out in the yard, when I heard a noise and I went to look - and he had tried to jump the wall, attempting to get to the herd of dairy cows in the next field - but he was teetering on top of it on his tummy! Honestly. Eventually he made it right over the wall, fell on his head and bent his neck right back. I thought he'd broken his neck, but no, not a bit of it. He got up and went careering down the field towards the cows that were out there, scattering them all over the place… And that's what really decided the old man to send him to market as soon as possible.

So to market he went and I don't know what happened to that bull after that. Somebody else's problem.

Down to the Local

Gaffer had a couple of point-to-pointers and he used to have to have them exercised every day. Now this was not a very exciting job, y'know. Horses have to have at least two hours exercise each day keep them fit, and just walking a couple of horses for a couple of hours can cover a fair distance I can tell you! So this was a job that Frank, one of Gaffer's lads, was given - walking the horses every day that they weren't out hunting. Now, he might not have been very keen on it, but it was a paid job and it wasn't hard work.

One day, however, Frank had another job on and couldn't go 'walkies', so Gaffer did it himself that day.

So there he was, walking his horses through Callow End in the general direction of the Old Hills and passing The Bluebell pub on his right, when the two horses tugged at the reins. Strange, he thought, what do they want? So he gave them their head and they turned into the pub drive. Stranger and stranger – and he let them go to see what would happen next. They both wandered around the back of the pub and expectantly waited at the back door……

Presumably they were used to getting a few tit-bits there while they waited for Frank to finish his pint!

Frank got the push that very afternoon.

The Blue Bell in Callow End

All Change: The Stonehouse Interim

One day we were out exercising the horses when Joan said that before long she'd have to go and look after her Mum and Dad because they weren't too good, especially her mother. She said she'd have to farm the place, which was Grange Farm nearby.   Would I go and help her? So of course I said yes, I would.

After all, I had nothing, I was foot loose and fancy free and so why not?

So, we were going to leave Gaffer Tolley's and go to Guarlford. However, we hadn't got to go there for about a year or so and this was when Gaffer was very helpful to us. He let us have a cottage and some land – The Stonehouse at Lower Woodsfield Farm on the Madresfield Estate – and we lived there for a time.

He even lent us tractors and a lorry when we needed it, and so forth.

The Stonehouse, at Lower Woodsfield Farm, with the Riley parked outside

So it was at The Stonehouse that we settled ourselves down and set ourselves up ready for moving to Grange Farm.

There was some land at the back of Stonehouse where we could have cattle and poultry, and of course we needed to be on the spot to keep an eye on the pullets. There was quite a bit of money to be made from rearing baby chicks to point-of-lay pullets in those days and we had 200 of them at one stage.

For a time we had a Rhode Island Red hen sitting on a nest of 12 duck eggs. On the Monday, Market Day, the eggs hadn't hatched, so we asked the Gaffer to get us a few day old ducklings, which he did. When we came to put them under the hen to our horror the eggs had hatched. This dear old hen lifted up her wing and accepted the ten other ducklings. How she covered them all I've no idea but she was a wonderful mother and reared all twenty two. When they grew to be adult she wouldn't be parted from them and if you went in there to catch a duck you took your life in your hands.

We also bought little calves and reared them up and sold them as little cattle, which gave us a start for when we came to Guarlford about a year later, in 1949.

Barkis

However, with all those pullets and over 20 heifers, we felt the need for rather more carrying capacity than either Joan's horse or my motorcycle. To be fair, we did still have the use of Gaffer's lorry occasionally, but the chance of having something of our own was very appealing.....

Despite having no car of his own at the time, Joan's brother, Colin, found us an open four-seater 1928 Riley 9 Lynx (WL 6673). This proved to be a quite reliable and very game old jalopy, and we called it Barkis*.

Jo with her mother in Barkis, in Wales

Colin naturally gave the Riley a once-over outside his house in Brixton, before driving it across on a Friday to deliver it to us in Malvern. However, it wasn't quite that simple though, as Colin's wife and son, Peggy and John, were way up north in Scarborough visiting her father Jack and some of her friends, so setting out very early on the Saturday morning, Colin and ourselves headed up to Yorkshire in our 'new car'.

Now, this was quite an unusual thing for us as we couldn't just leave the farm of course, but we had a trusted friend, a retired cow-man in the village, and he agreed to look after things for a couple of days. It proved to be a bright summer's day and Joan could clearly remember us briskly driving through the Yorkshire Dales with the stone walls flashing just past her left elbow.....

Anyway, we enjoyed visiting the attractive east-coast resort for the first and possibly the only time, but we soon headed back south on Sunday afternoon, and this time rather heavily laden with Colin and myself up front, and Joan and Peggy behind, with John sandwiched between them. Nevertheless, we made it down to London to Colin & Peggy's house in Brixton safely. We stayed there overnight and got up for an early start the next morning. Not difficult when you are regularly used to getting the milking done well before breakfast, so perhaps a 6am start was not actually that early a start for us after all. Anyway, we were off for the final leg back to Guarlford and all went well for our first adventure in Barkis.

It helped us with the farm work too. We used that first car for all sorts of things - for towing hen-houses across fields, collecting bags of grain from Worcester and towing trailers full of calves to market. It was a fine car was Barkis - it would go up from Guarlford all the way to the Wyche Cutting (on the crest of the Malvern Hills) in top gear - something that no modern car I've had would do!

* **Barkis.** Earned its Dickensian nickname, from *David Copperfield*, because *"Barkis is willin', ye-es, Barkis is willin'!"*

Working at Grange Farm

Once we had settled into Grange Farm, Joan and I took over the major part of running it on Pop's behalf. Pop was Victor Bradshaw, Joan's father, while his wife, Floss, was called Mother by Joan & Colin, but was referred to as 'Mrs. B' by me. She was a lovely lady and we got on very well and became the best of friends. By the 1950s, however, Pop was finding farming's physical work rather too much, which is why he was happy to let Joan & me take over.

We soon bought our own cow with the money from the little cattle and then another cow from the first milk cheque, and so we went on. You certainly couldn't do that nowadays, but in those days you could. Things were much easier then and there was hardly any red tape at all - you could just do what you liked when you liked. So this was how we built up a good herd of cows.

Then we had sheep too, which we used to lamb down and then sell. We'd buy more in the autumn, run them through the winter and lamb them down and sell them on. One really strange happening with the sheep that I can remember very clearly was that one day I brought the sheep up past the barn where my alsation, Judy, was lying up on the bales minding her own business, when all of a sudden one of the ewes took off up the bales like a mountain goat. Judy took one look and fled for dear life with the ewe in hot pursuit. She chased Judy round and round the long building with the rest of the flock looking on petrified. Eventually the ewe ran out of steam and gave up the chase.

Another occasion when we were in the middle of lambing at about three in the morning, we had a ewe in difficulty and we just could not get the lambs. So I went to fetch Charlie Williams, a friend and neighbour. I threw some gravel up at his bedroom window and a head appeared. I told Charlie the trouble and he said *"Hang on kid"* and came out doing his buttons up. We came back to the farm and he managed to get the lambs out alright. I believe farmers used to take difficult lambings to Charlie in the back of their Land-Rovers.

There was always at least one horse about the place of course, and Mrs. B always made a fuss of them, as she did with all the animals.

Mrs. B with Joan's Robin, while Pop can just be seen to the right, behind the fence.

34

Pigs to the Slaughter

We had pigs. Oh – and we had some adventures with pigs I can tell you. We bought one cock-eared pig from Ledbury Market, and when she was out she wanted to be in, and when she was in she wanted to be out. So we put up an electric fence of two strands and made a pen for her outside in the orchard at the back of the house - and ten minutes later she was out. We couldn't think how she did this, so we mended the wire and stood back and looked...... She just stood back and charged the wires, squealing all the time, and of course the wire broke and out she went, her and all the little piglets. She got out and went down the road and - oh she was a nightmare!

We were in market on the Monday and we saw a pig harness, so we thought 'Oh <u>that</u>'ll settle her*!'* We brought this home and on Sunday morning Bill Sims came over to help us put this harness on the pig. Well, we got it on and she stood and squealed and squealed and squealed and everybody was putting their heads over the fence saying *"What're you doing to that pig?"* So we had to take it off in the end.

"This is enough, I've had this pig up to my ears, she's going to market" I said to Joan. So on Monday morning we put her in the trailer and off to market she went. We sold her to George Yardley, Bill's son.

I saw George about a month later and asked him *"How d'you get on with the pig?"*

"Don't you mention that bloody pig to me! he said to me. *"It wrecked a brand new pig ark - and now it's sausages."* So that was the end of that.

In the early days just after the war - and people would be horrified by this now - but in the '30s and right up until the early '50s, the butchers in The Shambles in Worcester just used to go down to Market on a Monday, buy their cattle and bring them back, unload them and then they'd be slaughtered on the spot. They all had small slaughterhouses at the back of the shops, so the new cattle could clearly see what was coming! When you think about it now, there would be 'shock-horror' wouldn't there? That just wouldn't be allowed. You can imagine all the mamby pamby people that there are about nowadays, all having forty fits.

Back in those days, though, we just took it all as it came. For example, one morning I went in to feed one of the sows with her piglets and there was a little piglet lying there, all blue. I thought *'Oh dear, she's lain on it and killed it'.* They did that sometimes. Joan was squaring up the muck-bury outside - it was quite high and had got  very hot inside, decomposing and brewing very well. So I chucked this piglet up on the muck-bury and said to Joan *"Bury that while you're up there, will you."* With that, it jumped up and squealed blue murder! As the little pig landed, it must have knocked the breath back into it, and so it ran the length of the muck-bury, down and onto the ground and went shrieking up and down the yard! And of course by then the sow was going mad about her piglet, which got all her other piglets excited too. I had to let her out before she broke out and so we had this sow and all her little pigs galloping up and down the yard, all squealing their heads off.

By that stage we were no better than them – we were absolutely helpless with laughter, we just collapsed.... It was so funny with these little pigs and their tiny legs all going like lightening and such a noise! – all hell was let loose. Eventually we got them all back in of course, but it was a good story for an evening for a long time afterwards.

Some time later a chap called Voyce came over because he wanted to buy two gilts from us. So we took him round and then he wanted to see all the pigs we'd got. So we showed him all the pigs. He'd come at six at night and he eventually went home about eleven o'clock and by then he'd bought every pig we'd got on the place. We'd spent half an hour or more arguing about half a crown a head, but in the end he agreed to give us half a crown if we'd deliver them. So we delivered them with Gaffer Tolley's lorry - and when we got there we had to go and see all his pigs of course..... And then it was "*Come in and have a drink*" while he paid us - he gave us a cheque - and he also gave us another drink, but then he said "*Just before you go you must try this*" and bought out yet another bottle. It was gooseberry wine and it was absolutely beautiful, but when we got in the fresh air we wished we hadn't. Oh dear, oh dear.... It was in the days before the breathalyser, thank goodness, and by then it was quite late at night so there was nobody about much - in those days nobody moved much after ten o'clock at night - and we got home alright.

So that was the end of another episode - and that was the end of the pigs too. We never had any more pigs after that.

Holidays

It was mainly a 7-day working week for us at that time, but we did manage a second whole weekend away. We drove in the Riley up to Town to visit Colin & Peggy once again. However, the magneto packed up just outside Henley.

In those days, it wasn't unusual to carry a spare magneto in the toolbox, just in case. All sorts of spares, really. I don't know quite why I did it, but I do remember saying to Joan, just before we left, "*I think I'll pop that spare mag into the back, just in case.....*"

However, fitting and timing it was a bit of a job, but our luck came up trumps and a passing lorry stopped to help - and towed us into Henley - where there was a Riley Agent who was happy to help fit and time the magneto and get us going again! People could look after themselves in those days, despite us being smartly dressed for a night's entertainment in the big city! (Joan had been particularly pleased with her new honey-coloured dress as I remember.)

But by this time we were feeling a little grubby and well behind schedule, so I put my foot down and we were soon roaring round Marble Arch and over the river to pick Colin & Peggy up in Brixton. I wouldn't want to do that now, not in London today! Anyway, there they were, hanging out of the upstairs window watching for us. We got washed and tidied up – with Colin doing his best to remove grease from Joan's dress with a petrol-soaked rag.

"*His 'cure' made it worse and I stank of petrol all night!*" added Joan. Unsurprisingly, I was exhausted, what with all the fuss and driving through London for the first time since the war, so I tossed the keys across to Colin.

"*You can drive, Colin, because you know the way and I don't!*"

We were soon all off in time to just make the start of the show* - and we even got to park nearby in the Air Ministry car park, where Colin worked!

*Show   It was '*Let's Face It*', a musical comedy with Bobby Howes at the London Hippodrome in the West End.

Actor Bobby Howes

Hunting and Point-to-Point

We were hunting still of course – we were younger then and made time for it, you know. One time Joan and I were cantering side by side along the side of a wood and a tree had blown down in the gale. It was a huge root and both the horses, for no reason at all, decided that it was something dangerous there. They did a terrific shy sideways and Joan and I went straight on…. We landed on our backs, side by side. Len, Chug and Jo Fellows were behind us and had seen it all - they nearly fell off their horses laughing at us. That was the first time we finished up side by side. Then another day I was coming out of a field, onto a road, through a gap - and they say you should never go through a gap, you should always jump the hedge - but it was onto the road so everyone was going through the gap. My horse decided that there wasn't a gap, it was all hedge, and jumped high enough to clear the hedge and had me off, which can happen quite easily if you are not expecting it. We call it getting 'jumped off'. So Joan behind me was laughing at me lying on my back in the road - and then her horse did exactly the same thing and we ended up side by side on the road again. Everybody thought it was hilarious.

One winter it was particularly frosty, but the roads were dry and so as long as we kept on the roads we were fine, but all the verges were icy. As we went past Newland Grange Farm they started up a saw-bench and put a big, wet log on it. It suddenly shrieked and squealed really loudly.

Of course the horses did a terrific shy sideways and off we came - side by side on the side of the road, yet again. Away went the horses, but fortunately in those good old days there used to be men hedging and ditching and one fellow caught the horses for us. We went running down the road dreading what we'd find, but there they were safe and sound.

Those were the episodes you could really have done without but they were quite amusing at the time.

Joan rode in a couple of Point-to-Points. Theoretically, we couldn't ride in those events if you were working with horses because in those days that classed you as 'professionals', but Joan did manage to get a ride at Bushley on a mare that we had at the time, called Carlisle Bay, that I've mentioned before. Harold Tolley said she should follow a certain horse, I can't remember its name now, but he said follow that one because it's very experienced and it won't fall. So Joan followed this horse and, of course, it fell at the first fence didn't it. Joan's horse was one of those that hadn't got what we call a 'fifth leg' and crumpled up and chucked Joan off. She dislocated her shoulder, which is more trouble really than a broken collarbone.

We used to have terrific fun taking them for gallops though. If the weather was bad down here we used to go up on Bredon Hill. It was wonderful up there because the going was so good and you could even jump the odd wall if nobody was looking.

As I mentioned before, we also used to go to Worcester Racecourse sometimes. About six of us would go and have a school round there. All above board it was, and great fun too.

Then Joan rode at Chaddesley Corbett. She rode Robin Adair there, and Robin never fell, so she survived that and I think she was about third or fourth.

Joan and Robin Adair

Both Joan and I enjoyed hunting and eventing - and with some success too! Amongst our more memorable horses were Laddie, Timmy, Glory-Be, Burtie, Billy, Donegal and Robin Adair. Robin was a particularly successful point-to-pointer and Robin with Len Chugg on top won the Croome Farmers' Race in 1946, amongst many others.

Then there was Jakey and many others too….. but you'll have to wait until Chapter 8 for more about them.

Joan on Glory-Be and Jo on Burtie

Joan on Donegal

Press photo

We were still using horses on the farm of course, even after we'd got the Fergie Grey tractor.

Joan taking nephew John for a ride at Grange Farm, 1952

Friends

We made a lot of friends at that time, including Mr. & Mrs Smith and their daughter Meriel. They lived at Guarlford Court at the time, directly opposite Grange Farm and where Joan and her brother Colin used to live. Meriel remembers an event from those days.

"When I was only about nine years old, my father suffered near fatal arsenic poisoning and was seriously ill for several days. During this time Jo took on the task of milking our cows, which was no mean undertaking with her own livestock to care for at Grange Farm."

There was also Bob Rouse who did our haulage and used to bring us the odd horse, including Burtie.

Just around the corner, Bill and Rene Simms were good friends too, and then they had a daughter, Catherine. Little was I to know just how much Cath was to contribute to our lives over the next sixty years.

Jo and baby Catherine outside the house at Grange Farm

And then there was Verity Pease, a neighbouring farmer who had a Point-to-Pointer, and we were her back-up team on occasion. It was Verity who rescued me one time, after I'd been hunting and gone through a gap in the hedge and my horse's leg caught a bit of barbed wire and fell, throwing me and resulting in a bad cut on my forehead. Oh, I knew not to go through a gap – I should have jumped the hedge, but that's what I did, and got punished for it. But Verity got to me quickly, bleeding like a stuck pig, and bandaged me up. Then she got me and my horse back home in her horsebox and looked after us until Joan took over. (Sadly my horse was hurt too and he ended up with a hematoma between his front legs.)

Another day, I seemed to have upset Verity. I don't know what I'd done, but she was cross – oh she was cross. I told Joan about it all.

"I've really upset her for some reason – that's the end of a beautiful friendship I suppose...." I said. Anyway, about two days later, Joan and I were repairing some fencing down in the field and we saw Verity walking towards us....

"Bloody hell – she's come to have another go at me!" She came right up to me - and apologised!

"I'm so sorry Jo. I was awfully bad tempered and quite unreasonable, so here's a bottle of whisky to try to make up." And so we stayed the best of friends from then on.

Harry and Humphrey Bladder were near neighbours, at Fowlers Farm, where Humphrey still lives. They had a petrol pump out front and we used to fill Barkis up there. They even helped us push-start the old car afterwards as well! In fact, it's still there and the remains of the pump can still be seen in the ramshackle shed, on the road from Guarlford to the Rhydd, but there's no petrol left in it, I'll bet!

I can remember going with Harry and Humphrey down to get watercress off Longden Marsh, which was beautiful. It was lovely stuff. You can never buy anything like it nowadays, it had really thick stems and was peppery and absolutely lovely. You wouldn't even dare eat it now, out of the marsh, even if you could get it I suppose.

And then one day Humphrey phoned us up and Joan answered the 'phone.

"Miss Bradshaw, you and Miss Newell, you get your guns and come over here right now. We're cutting the corn and have got that bloody fox that's been at our hens trapped in the middle – between us we'll have the bugger when he comes out!"

So we went over, me with my grandfather's 12-bore which had a kick like a mule, but Joan didn't have one of course – she didn't carry a gun from way back when she'd shot Jimmy the ferret by mistake. So there we were, all spaced around the remaining patch of corn, each loaded and watching out, when Joan says to me:

"You just pray it doesn't come your way, won't you…" And I did. I didn't want to shoot a fox. It would have probably been wounded and it would have got away to die slowly.

We'd go down to the Bladders' each New Year and Nancy Bladder, Harry and Humphrey's mother, used to put on the most wonderful supper. She'd do excellent pickled pork. I've no idea how she did it, but it really was very special indeed. Not a supper to miss was the one at Fowlers Farm.

Joan on Billy and Jo on Jakey arriving home after a good ride

41

Chapter 5
SETTLING DOWN

Barns & Buildings

When we started on the farm we soon needed a barn – so we had to put one up ourselves. We knew of a firm, Smiths of Worcester, that had the framework of a barn, but no roof, so they came and put the framework up for us. We then had to put a roof on and so we needed some tin. Joan's brother, Colin, found us some at a reasonable price and so we went and collected this tin – corrugated iron, really – and, well, just put the roof on....

Humphrey Bladder came and helped me at nights, after he'd finished work on his own farm. We worked with a Tilley lamp hanging on each corner of the barn. I mean what a mad trick to do, it's a wonder we didn't break our necks! I used to go on in the daytime, but Joan hadn't got any head for heights so she'd come about half way up the ladder with a cup of coffee for me. Eventually we got the roof on the barn and it's still there now, over fifty years later, I'm pleased to say.

I remember sitting up there putting the ridge on, hammering the big nails in, all on my own.... Anyway we survived, God looked after us I suppose, or somebody did.

Jo and Joan, with Judy the Alsatian, Jo's first dog.
To the left is the very recently built barn.

43

That's the same barn on the right as you go into the Nursery today, and when I look up at it nowadays I think to myself 'Dear God! - I wouldn't go up there now for a thousand pounds!'

Jo, Carol and the original Barn.   Christmas Eve, 2011

Photo by John

Between us Joan and I also built the buildings round the back, attached to the big barn and we built the brick walls too. When you farm and you haven't got a lot of money you have to become a 'jack of all trades', which we did. We enjoyed it - it was all very interesting.

We even learned how to lay a hedge later!   All sorts of things we did.

The Barn Despite having survived very well for over 50 years, the barn has weakened and so Carol is having to replace it. However, she is waiting until after Jo's book-launch at the Nursery. The new barn will be in much the same style, in order to retain the overall appearance of the site.

Little Boys with Sticks

When we were on a short holiday down in Hampshire we went to the sale of the New Forest ponies down at Beaulieu Road. We were really shocked and horrified by the way they were treated. There were small pens about 8x6 feet, where they were packed in, mares & foals, yearlings, two year olds, stallions - all the lot, all together. As soon as they filled one pen they'd fill another - and there seemed to be dozens of little boys with sticks.....

In the ring, it was quite a big ring, but was halved by the amount of men all round it, each with a stick as well. The ponies were smacked with sticks by the kids all the way to the ring and as soon as they came into the ring these men were hitting them as they went by on the rump and the poor things were absolutely terrified!

Anyway we went to look for the RSPCA man who was in the bar and wasn't at all concerned, and he said *"Well, they're just wild ponies."*

"Yeh, and they're making them a lot wilder!" I said, and then we went to the auctioneers, but they just echoed him.

So we went home and wrote to the RSPCA and suggested that they went to see the sale of the real wild ponies off the mountains in Wales, sold by a chap called Michael Wyatt, at Hay. There the treatment was totally different. They were all in individual pens, mares and foals, yearlings, two year olds and stallions kept completely separate. They were just put into the ring quietly, no shouting and no sticks. In the ring was one man, with a stick with a little bit of white cloth on the end of it. He just got the ponies moving round the ring very quietly. Michael Wyatt would tolerate nobody hitting the ponies and that's how the sales were run. So that's why we suggested that the Beaulieu Road people might take a lesson from that.

Having written to the RSPCA, we had a pompous, self-satisfied man come to see us. Obviously he'd come thinking we were a couple of silly, sentimental old women, and he was very patronising.

"Well you know these are wild ponies and so......" he said, and so on, yackety, yackety yack *".... and they have to be hit."*

"Rubbish! They don't have to be hit...." we said *" ..but if an animal needs a smack we can certainly give it a smack, but what was happening there was unforgivable. What's more, there were two or three other people there who thought exactly the same as we did."*

Again we suggested that he went to see how the pony sales at Hay on Wye were conducted, which was totally different - and I can tell you, those ponies are much wilder than the New Forest ponies!

Anyway, he finally climbed down off his perch and became quite reasonable in the end, and then he toddled off. Of course we had a letter from them to say that they were looking into it, and all the usual rubbish, but we didn't really expect anything to come of it.....

However, about twelve months later, on the front page of the *Horse and Hound*, was a great big picture of the New Sale Rings at Beaulieu Road - with just one man in there and with a stick with a white flag on it! There were no kids with sticks, and the pens were all occupied by mares & foals, and yearlings, two year olds and three year olds all on their own, with the stallions separated.

So I suppose they must have paid a visit to Hay on Wye, to see how it was done. So that was a bit of success.

There was another incident very similar, but this was Joan's good deed really. She took some cattle to Gloucester Market one day, and when she got there she was horrified because there again were little boys with sticks hitting everything they could find to hit, and nobody was doing anything about it.

So she went to the auctioneers' office to complain and they said there wasn't much they could do about it.

"*Well, until you <u>do</u> do something about it, I'm not moving the lorry....*" she told them, and took the key out of her lorry and walked away. So they were all stuck. Nobody could get in or out, because you went in one end and through, unloaded the cattle and then turned round and came back out the same way. But not with Joan's lorry there you didn't.....

Then the policeman came over to her to sort things out.

"*Well, you really must move it, y'know miss......*" he said, but Joan said that she wasn't going to until something was done about hitting the animals. And then the dealers came round, all in a tiz they were.

"*You <u>gotta</u> move that! You can't just leave it there, in our way it is. You gotta move it.*"

"*I'm not going to*" said Joan again, digging her heels in. So in the end they chased all the kids out and Joan moved the lorry.

In the meantime the Auctioneer had rung Gaffer Tolley to give him a bit of his mind.

"*Don't you send that girl again*" he told Mr.Tolley, "*She's just trouble, she is!*" and he told our Gaffer why, in some detail.   But the Gaffer wasn't going to be told what to do and he stuck up for Joan.

"*Well, she was quite right, you shouldn't allow those kids in there.*" - but the Auctioneer still told him he was not to send her again.......

Being the Gaffer, he sent her again the very next week. The officials took one look at Joan and said to the kids "*Hop it!*"

So I think that after that the little boys were kept out of the market, and so that was another good thing that Joan achieved.

*Jo and Joan at the
Three Counties Show
in the 1950s*

Sheep and Calves

Each year, we used to try to get the lambing over in a couple of weeks, but it was a case of nights up and popping out to see how they were, and popping back to have a warm up because it was usually freezing cold, or wet or something. We used to make little pens to put them in as they lambed, or bring them in if we could.

Then one day, I think we'd been hunting, we came back and it started to sleet. The ewes and lambs were out in the field at the back and we thought, '*Oh Lord, we can't leave them out in that!*' The lambs had got their backs up and they looked really miserable. We'd got a long wooden shed at the back of the barn in which we had turkeys at Christmas, so we put some bales of straw in there and tied some hurdles up and put some hay behind them and put some water in there and I went down to fetch these sheep. For some reason we couldn't bring them in through the gateway at the top, I think it was too muddy with the cows going in and out. So I brought them up the road - and it was ever so funny. I got them out onto the road and they just took off. They shot off up the road and I had to run up and follow them in through the gate, up past the barn, round the corner at the top and into the shed they went – just as if they knew where they were going.

We went back about half an hour later and most of the ewes were either lying down or eating hay and the lambs were either lying down asleep or playing and we stood there and watched them. It was so satisfying to see them so happy and content and warm and dry. So we brought them in for lambing evermore after that, and ours never lambed out again, which was much better for us and for them.

Also you have to trim sheep's feet, which entails catching hold of the ewe and sitting her up on her tail. Once you've got the knack of it it's quite easy, but until you get the knack it's darned hard. Their feet are quite hard too and also you have to what we call "dagg" them, which means cutting out mucky wool from round their tails and then their backs – down their hind legs, to keep them clean and to stop any danger of maggots which of course will get in anywhere like that. Keeping sheep wasn't easy.

Then we used to calve the cows. We very rarely had any trouble, because usually they managed it all on their own. Occasionally, though, you'd have to give one a bit of a hand. I have to tell you in those days there were no rubber gloves, you had to get on with it and get your hand right in there and put up with it. With hot soapy water hopefully. And a good, hot, bath afterwards.

But there was one cow we had that we just couldn't get the calf out - we knew something was radically wrong. So we rang the vet, it was Les Harries from Upton, and he came up.

"*Well she's gone too far for a Caesarean, and the calf's dead anyway, so I'll have to cut it up in the cow, because we just can't get it out any other way.*" So he stripped off to the waist - it was freezing cold - and he said "*Well - one of you will just have to help me.*"

Joan quickly vanished, saying "*I'll just go and do the milking....*"

This was about seven in the morning. He cut this calf up inside the cow and he was bringing out the first leg when - but I won't go into all the gory details here....

That was one of the worst calvings I ever did experience and I must admit I don't think I had any breakfast that morning.

But it's just one of those things you have to get on with and do it when the situation arises. I'm sure nothing's changed for farmers today in that respect.

We used to help each other out – well, we needed to. In the winter, or when times were bad, we'd pull together.

The winter of 1981 was bad, for example. I remember we helped out a bit, but Meriel Bennett remembers that time in particular:

"It was a very severe winter, but all I had was a Mini pickup and that was no use with the amount of snow on the local roads. So Jo came to the rescue with her Land-Rover and horsebox. She took me to Midland Shire Farmers to collect our animal feed and then to Cygnet Lodge Farm in Hanley Swan to collect a calf I'd bought as an additional one for a freshly calved cow – and that wouldn't wait! I cannot imagine how I would have managed without Jo's help. We were all struggling to cope that winter and each day was long, arduous and stressful – but Jo didn't hesitate to offer practical assistance."

Building a haystack:
Jo and Bob Jones up top, and Joan throwing it up to them.

More Cows

We had a cow called Mary who was the first that we'd bought with the return from the calves and then we had one called Tilley who was a very, very pretty cow. She was a Jersey/Frisian cross and was black with a brownish tinge to her coat. She had the mealy muzzle of a Jersey and was a very pretty little cow all round. She gave a wonderful lot of milk and was the sweetest natured thing you could ever hope to meet - except when she calved. When she

calved she became an absolute so and so. She even pinned me against the wall one day - and she'd got horns too! I was very lucky not to get injured, so after that we had all their horns off. Of course you don't see horned cows now except for the Old English cattle. She used to get milk fever every time, which is a lack of calcium, and its amazing how the cow staggers around and then goes down flat out and you think, '*Oh my God she's going to die!*' but the vet comes along and gives them this bottle full and they're up in seconds and right as ninepence. It was really quite extraordinary, but very frightening at the time.

Then we had one that used to jump. A bit like the mad bull that Gaffer Tolley had - she could jump everything. She'd jump the electric fence wire, she'd jump a gate, she'd jump here and she'd jump there. So we sold her to a chap up on Poolbrook Common who turned her out on the common and we thought '*Oh - she won't stop there five minutes!*' - but she did.

He had no problem with her at all - obviously she just didn't like being confined.

Jo with Judy and her pups in about 1954, with Catherine Simms, later Cath Lockley

One day I was stripping out Mary, which you do before you put the milking machine on - you just draw a bit of fore-milk - when the heifer standing beside her kicked me in the back. I went straight on my face, my head in between Mary's front legs. Fortunately she was a lovely, stately old dame and didn't move a muscle. But the heifer jumped all over my back and my thighs and I was yelling blue murder for Joan, who was in the dairy and couldn't hear me. Cath's uncle, her mother's brother, heard me and came running in and shouted "*Jo's in trouble!*"

Well, by the time they got to me I'd already got myself out. The heifer had jumped back and I had managed to get to my feet, but I was battered all over. Joan took me straight back to the house and into a hot bath to stew for a good time, probably with a tot of whisky to get me by, but before very long I was black and blue all over my back and sides.

It was something I could have well done without, I can tell you.

And Horses – There's Always Horses!

All through this, we always found time for our horses, and other people's too. In fact, as the years went by, there were more horses belonging to others than were ours, but I'll tell you more about that later on.

Joan and Harry Bladder bringing a couple of horses in from the back paddock.

Jo and Harry having just unloaded Lyndora from their Rice horse-box, towed by the Ford Consul (which Jo later sold to Joan's brother, Colin)

Chapter 6
BUILDING ON PAST EXPERIENCES

A Nasty Blow

In 1959 I had an accident. Well, two really. First, I came off a horse going down a bank at a schooling gallop. We were turning left and my horse, a little mare, ducked out to the right and I went straight on and hurt my back. I didn't think anything of it at the time.

So that wasn't so bad, but then I was working on a piece of equipment on the farm and it was held up by a long handle on a ratchet. I was bending over doing a repair to this piece of machinery and the ratchet slipped and it came down and hit me in the back. I really thought it had broken my back that time, it was awful - I don't think I've known anything so painful in my entire life.

Shortly afterwards, I was having breakfast one morning and I went to get up - and I simply couldn't move. I won't go into the long sad story of my back – I went here and they looked at it, I went there and they X-rayed it, but it didn't matter where I went, they couldn't fix it - and I was in agony all the time. I was really in a hell of a mess, because after that I had desperate back trouble for a long time and I had to give up farming because I just couldn't do it any more. I couldn't lift anything or I'd lock solid again - and I couldn't do anything with the animals, which is what really hurt. I mean, I couldn't milk cows, couldn't lift a bale of hay and Joan couldn't do it all of course. We couldn't afford to pay other people to do it either, because we weren't a big enough business.

We'd still got horses mind, and we still had a few animals about. We ran some beef cattle which were easy to look after, and sheep too, but we had to get rid of the dairy cows. That's what really caused the financial trouble

RRE – Driving Again

So I thought, what else could I do? I could drive. So we sold the cows and I went and got a job driving for the Air Ministry, up at the RRE*. I did that for about eight years, while Joan ran the farm with beef cattle, which I could help her with in the evenings - when I was there, that is - and at weekends. We still had the sheep too, and one way and another we coped.

---

*RRE The RRE (Radar Research Establishment) was formed in 1953 by combining the TRE (Telecommunications Research Establishment), already located in Malvern, with the RRDE (Radar Research & Development Establishment). It was re-labelled the Royal Radar Establishment in 1953.
In 1976 it merged with the SRDE (Signals Research & Development Establishment) to form the RSRE (Royal Signals Research Establishment).
Initially within the Ministry of Aviation, then the Ministry of Technology and finally the Ministry of Defence, it was then privatised in 2001 to form part of QinetiQ.

TRE Malvern huts in winter 1942-3

The job at RRE was quite interesting. I was in the Official Car Service* and I used to ferry people around, often scientists, from Malvern to meetings all over the place. The hours were often very long, and we wore a green uniform with a forage cap - a bit like the army, so I felt quite at home. We used to go near and far, to Pershore and Defford, and to Stevenage, Chelmsford, Fylingdales, all over the shop.

OCS Humber Super Snipe cars and their drivers. Jo particularly disliked this car.

Chelmsford was quite a long journey in those days, about four and a half hours or so. I'd have to start off at about six in the morning and get back at, well, any time of night really. Sometimes I used to have to take them to catch an early plane at an airport and pick them up coming back from wherever in the world they'd been.

One night I went to pick up some people at the airport. When I went to that particular airport, I used to park down the side of Number 4 Building and had done that for years. I collected my passengers and we went back to the car - and the car had gone! *'Oh God! I don't believe it...!'* I thought. I'd left my requisition sheet and my uniform cap on the seat. There was a policeman there and so I told him and he said *"Oh, it'll be in the Pound, about 3 miles away...."* My passengers and I got a taxi to the Airport Pound and, true enough, there was my car. I went stamping up to the sergeant who was taking all the particulars and I asked him what it was all about - we'd been parking there for years! He took not a bit of notice and just went on writing. Finally he looked up and said *"That'll be three pounds."* So I had to give him three quid and got my car back.

I did eventually get my three quid back too, but from the Union, not the Service.

---

*__Official Car Service__ The Mechanised Transport Corps (MTC) was formed in 1939 as a women's voluntary organisation, later adopted by the Ministry of War Transport to provide Staff Car drivers, so it had a lot in common with the ATS in which Jo had served, but was otherwise unconnected.
The Official Car Service (OCS) was then formed in 1946 by merging the fleet of cars in the Ministry of Aircraft Production with that in the MTC and put under the control of the Ministry of Supply.
While the OCS had originally been formed to ferry Ministers, officials, military leaders and assorted VIPs around, it also safely transported the government's scientists, the 'Back-Rooms Boys', from laboratories to testing grounds and to meetings. However, the emphasis was always centred on Whitehall, and in 1952 it was re-labelled the Government Car Service.
Nevertheless, away from London it was usually still called the OCS, which is how Jo remembers it.

Fit to Burst

Then another day I was driving a chap to a meeting, down through Morton in Marsh and out the other side, on the Oxford road just over the railway bridge. Suddenly my passenger, who was in the seat next to me, went "*Aaaagh!*" and threw his arm out across my chest! I stopped dead – he'd frightened me to death. '*What the hell's the matter with him?*' I thought.

So I got out of the car and went round to his side, and there he was, lying back making awful noises.... There was a woman cleaning windows nearby and I shouted to her.

"*Quick - come and help me please!*" She came running over and took one look at him.

"*Oh, he's had a fit. Get him to a doctor. I'll come with you – I know the way.*" So she got into the back of the car and held his head while I turned the car round and shot off down the road. She knew where the doctors' surgery was and so I stopped there, leaving her in the car with him. I shot into the surgery's waiting room, all of a panic.

"*Where's the doctor?*" and they pointed and I said to the doctor "*Can you come – it's an emergency!*" He came running at the double, had a good look and agreed with the woman.

"*Oh it's all right, don't worry, he's just had a fit.*"

"*I'm sorry I barged in, but I thought he was dying....*" I said, but he was very nice.

"*Oh that's perfectly all right, don't worry. I'll ring the hospital.*" He then said to the window cleaning woman, who was still in the back of my car, "*Well, you know where the hospital is, don't you? - you'll be able to show the way.*"

When we got to the little cottage hospital, they were outside waiting for us - two nurses, and a stretcher trolley. They put him on and wheeled him into the hospital, saying to come back in two hours. So I took the helpful lady back home in the meantime and she said asked me in for a cup of coffee. I went in and we sat there nattering for about an hour or so and then I took myself out of her way. I went back to the hospital and by that time the scientist chap was a bit better, but not much. It must have been a very bad attack. So the doctor told me to go back again at lunch time. My day's itinerary was well and truly messed up by then so I rang my boss, Mr.Burns, to tell him.

"*You're to bring him straight back to us in Malvern – immediately!*" he told me. So I went back to the hospital at midday to get him, but this chap wouldn't have it at all.

"*Oh no!*" he said, "*I must go on, it's a very important meeting. I've got to go on.*" I told him that Mr. Burns had said that I'd got to take him home, but he asked the nurse for a 'phone and he rang Mr. Burns, who I assume told him to return to Malvern. So he handed the phone to me and Mr. Burns told me to take him back. So he was discharged and off we set for Malvern.

"*He won't have another fit now, don't you worry*" they all assured me.

So we got to Hanley Castle and he had another fit. I zoomed into the forecourt of the Post Office that was there in those days, jumped out and dashed in. A dear old boy ran it and I told him what had happened. He passed me his telephone and went out to see him.

"*You're not going to believe this, but he's had another fit. We're at Hanley Castle.*" There was a deathly pause at the other end of the line, and then Mr.Burns said

"*Oh my God.....You stay put, don't move and I'll get an ambulance down to you straight away.*" I have to say that in under fifteen minutes the ambulance came charging down the road, bells ringing, and they got him in and took him away as quick as anything.

Of course I had to go and see my boss when I got back and give him a full report of what had happened. He summed it all up for me.

"*He shouldn't have been in a car. People suffering from epilepsy are not allowed in a Ministry car on their own and they are certainly not allowed to travel in the front. He should have been with two more and they should have had him between them in the back.*"

Fair enough, I thought - I was glad to see the end of that!

Well damn me if about a month later I had to drive him again! But this time he was with three others: two sat in the back with him between them and one sat in the front with me. He was actually a very nice fellow and I felt terribly sorry for him, especially when he apologised and explained it all to me.

"I do apologise, Joan. I live next door to a fellow who suffers from shell-shock from the war and the night before he was ranting all around the house - and I'd had no sleep at all because of all the noise. I'm afraid that I got up in the morning and dashed off to work and forgot to take my medication and that's why I had those fits. I'm so sorry."

But I can tell you it was pretty frightening at the time for me, because I'd never seen anybody in a fit before. I was told that you should push them out of the car, onto the grass verge. Well, that's all very well if there's a grass verge, but what if there isn't? So I don't know what I should have done really. Very difficult.

Fog

Then one time I had a trip down to Stevenage in thick, thick fog. I don't think I've ever been in such a fog outside London, it was nearly as bad as the smog I'd experienced there during the war. We ran into the fog near Deddington on the Cotswolds and it took us about six hours to get to Stevenage. It was an absolute pea-souper.

There were two of us on that trip, Irish Anne Jones and myself and in the two cars there were five or six gentlemen, who were VIPs, or in fact SPSOs (Senior Principal Scientific Officers). We got them to their hotel safely and then Anne and I had to go about a mile back to where we were staying in a pub.

So we set off in my car, but by then we really couldn't see a thing in the dark, but just then a car went by, heading in the right direction for us, and so I latched onto him - although he was going like the clappers. He turned right where we'd got to turn, I did know that much, so that was good, but then he absolutely shot along this road.

"It's no good, I can't keep up with this because all I can see are his red tail-lights - and if he runs into anything we'll be straight into the back of him!" I said to Anne.

We were so close as to be able to keep him in sight, and it seemed as if we were only about six foot away, although it must have been more really. Anyway I slowed down a bit and we groped our way along - and sure enough, there he was in the ditch. So I'm afraid to say we left him there.....

The next morning dawned beautifully sunny, with no trace of the previous day's fog. We went off back to pick up the Very Important Passengers and take them to their meeting, a mile or two away from their hotel. We were supposed to pick them up at four o'clock from there, but they thought different.

"Well, in view of the awful weather, we shall be ready at two. We'll get home in the daylight, if you don't mind?"

Well, it was sunny and clear for the rest of the day, but nevertheless we did pick them up at 2pm as they wanted and we were back to Malvern two hours early.

Which was fine by us of course.

Tomlin's Tours

There was one chap we used to drive for, called Mr.Tomlin, who used to go off on business all around England - we called them 'Tomlin's Tours'. One winter I drove him for a whole week and by the end I'd done over eleven hundred miles - and every mile was in the dark, except for the morning we'd set off. He'd finish his day's meeting and we'd set off at about five o'clock at night, with probably about two hundred miles to do in order to get to our next port of call.

We went down to Norfolk and stayed the night there and then the next night he came out at about half past five and we'd got to go up to Yorkshire. I can't remember where we went next, but I do know where we were staying on the last night. We came back west from up on the East Coast, right across the country, and went up the big hill, Sutton Bank. We came up the hill and ran straight into thick fog. In the Yorkshire Moors in those days there weren't any cats eyes because of the snow ploughs. So there we were in this thick fog and there's no kerb, just grass edges. Mr.Tomlin had his head out of the window saying *"Right hand down a bit, more.... No! Left hand down a bit. OK, keep going straight."* We were hours getting there, when we should have been there in about an hour. We finally got to the pub where we were staying, very, very late, and bless their hearts they still cooked us a meal.

Then the next day, Friday, he went to Fylingdales and then we set off about six o'clock at night to come back to Malvern. I clocked in, left my requisition and headed for home. I'd had four 'working-after-midnight' journeys which meant that I got paid through till six o'clock the next morning. Except for the first 150/200 miles, I'd done that eleven hundred or more miles all in the dark, and we'd had rain, we'd had snow, we'd had fog and we'd had ice. Every concoction of weather you could think of, we'd had it that week.

I can tell you, by the time I got home it was about one o'clock in the morning and I was nearly dead on my feet. I went straight to bed and I think I stayed in bed all day Saturday. I just slept and slept and slept.....

Come Monday morning I went into work - I was not out on the road that day - and into the rest room walked George Gammage, Mr. Burns' assistant. He flung my requisition sheet onto the table.

"What bloody fiddle is this then?" he said loudly.

"You had better have words with Mr. Tomlin. He knows" I replied quietly. I got my full pay and that was the last I ever heard about it.

Then of course we had people who'd come out and say *"Oh I'm late, I've got to be there at so and so. Can you hurry please."* So we'd bust a gut to try to get them there in time – our risk, not theirs. But why didn't they just get up half an hour earlier?

Time after time that would happen, but there you are, there's nowt so queer as folk.

A New Role – and a New Friend

Quite out of the blue one morning, I was called into Jimmy Ashley's office - she was the Head Driver and our immediate boss, below Mr. Burns.

"We've got a new driver starting, she's called Rosemary Smith. She's got the makings of a good driver, but she needs a bit of advice and brushing up of her general driving skills." Well, I didn't like the sound of this, not at all.

"I'm not a driving instructor!" I said, but in the end I did take Rosie with me a couple of times and then she did some of the driving herself. It soon became clear that she was indeed a very good driver.

Rosie still remembers a little of this era, not so much the 'driving lessons', but particularly one 'amusing' bit early on:

"Jo had to deliver something to Bracknell – no passengers, so I was allowed to drive there. On the way back, however, Jo had her own agenda – she wanted to pick up an English Setter puppy she'd just bought. The pretty little thing was called 'Sue'. She was put on the back seat and I sat next to her as she was clearly nervous and unhappy about being taken away from home. Well, before very long it was quite clear that Sue was particularly unhappy about being in the back of a strange, squeaky clean new car. She was sick. All over the back seat.

So we had to stop, clear things up as best we could, and carry on. She was sick again, all over me this time. My new uniform took it all. We stopped again. And again.

Remember, we had to get back to RRE and book back in, and Jimmy knew roughly what time was allowed for our trip – and we had to drop the dog off at Guarlford first – and try to get rid of the smell - before we booked in ......

I think we only laughed about it afterwards."

Later on of course, Rosie was one of the team and went on trips on her own and with other drivers. She remembers fellow drivers Gladys Hall, Anne Jones, Margaret Miles, Marian Jones; as well as Jimmy's 'pets': George Farthing, George Scriven and Doug Goodwin.

"I can clearly remember one trip to Neatishead that Jo and I were sent on because, along with two others, one of the scientists in Jo's car was Tom McCarry. I can't remember who else was there or who was in my car, but Tom was the life and soul of the party and just loved practical jokes.

Well, we booked into the hotel – we were to be there for two nights – and after the meal and a couple of night-caps, Jo and I went up to our beds. Only to find that they were already occupied - by ashtrays. It just had to be one of Tom's jokes.

We didn't say anything about it over breakfast, but Jo and I got our own back – we sewed Tom's pyjama trouser legs up. The next morning he played the game and made no complaint at all, just the one comment:

'D'ye ken, it was so verrry warrm last night, I slept in the all-together, so I did.'
I wasn't to know it at the time of course, but Mac was eventually to be my father-in-law."

In conversation, I discovered that Rosie and I had a joint love of horses and dogs and that led onto far more than I had ever expected when Jimmy first told me to be a driving instructor!

Rosie explains why:

"My life long ambition was to ride a horse, right from a child that's all I wanted to do. But my parents were very strict and I was never even allowed to own a dog!"

In due course Rosie came down to the farm, along with Anne from Ireland who was a good friend of ours, and I introduced her to Joan and we all got on very well. This was the beginning of a friendship that was to last until the present day.

Rosie remembers her first ride and her horse:

"The two Joans soon put me up onto Sarah, a New Forest mare, out in the orchard with just a bridle and no saddle or even a helmet, and told me to 'get on with it'. I got on quite well - except when Sarah put her foot in a rabbit hole I went over her head. All Jo could say was 'Don't let go of the reins!' because Sarah was a bit of a devil to catch once she'd got away. I survived the fall and got back on.

After a few lessons, Jo told me that they couldn't teach me anything more so I'd better go up to the Avenue Riding School, at Barnards Green. I got on very well there and had lot of fun.

When I'd become a little more proficient, eventually Joan allowed me to ride her retired point-to-pointer, Robin, who, although quite old by that time, was still quite sparky. I really enjoyed that!

At that time I was living in a flat along the Worcester Road and then up in Malvern, but I was spending so much time down at Grange Farm that the two Joans said that I should just move in, so eventually I went to live at the farm for a bit. Until 1973 in fact, when I got married to Donald McCarry.

I can't remember at what point I thought I could have my own horse, but we saw an advert in the Malvern Gazette for a mare, an ex-race horse for £85. So the three of us went to look at her and we found her in an old railway truck, with no windows and not much room. She was a 15.3 hands dark bay, but as thin as a hat-rack, poor thing. She really was in very poor condition and we felt sorry for her – but I liked her too so I bought her.

She was officially called Hyperbond, by Hyperbole and Hyperion, but we called her Hypy.

As she progressed in health and me in skills, we got along very well. She was a wonderfully tempered mare and would do anything for me, being really easy to ride - we had lots of fun together. We took part in some local competition, y'know the sort of thing, dressage, jumping - oh but Hypy was good at hunting too - she just loved it and she took me with her! I just sat there and enjoyed it. We were with the Croome Hunt.

After her back injury, Jo had lost some of her confidence in riding, but she got on Hypy, who would never do anything wicked like throwing you off or anything, so Jo got back to riding again thanks to Hypy.

Of course, Jo then got Jakey, also an ex-race horse, and he was a different cup of tea altogether – he was full of naughtiness and a one-woman horse - nobody else could ride him!

Jo and I, with Jakey and Hypy, had a lot of fun together, including a Long Distance Ride. in the Forest of Dean.

Sadly Hypy went lame towards the end of the Ride and so we didn't pass the Fitness Test at the end, but altogether it was a full day of jolly good fun."

There's lots more about Hypy and Jakey, and the Long Distance Ride, in Chapter 8.

Light at the End of the Tunnel

While I was still working at the RRE, we had a mare that was lame and we couldn't get her sorted out. In those days of course there weren't all the osteopaths and physiotherapists and reflexologists and chiropractors for people and animals like there are now, oh no, but there have always been people who could help if you knew who to ask and where to look. For example, there was an old farmer in Wales who'd got the gift of putting bones back and that sort of thing - he was an osteopath really I suppose, but he didn't call himself that of course. I mean, he wasn't qualified or anything, just clever.

And then we were told about Ronnie Lonsford so we took the mare there and he said *"Oh - her pelvis is out...."* and he put it back and she was OK. Oh, he was clever too.

"Do you treat people as well?" I asked him.

"Maybe - what's your trouble? Bad back, by the look of you...." He'd seen it without me telling him, so I went into the house and he said *"Lie down on the floor"* and then he said *"You've got the same trouble as your mare!"*

"So why didn't the doctors find that then?" I said. *"They've X-rayed me and turned me inside out and upside down and still didn't see it!"* - but Ronnie knew.

"Because they don't look in the right place, in the right way". Anyway he treated it and for the first time in nine years I was out of pain. Then he told me how it would go: *"You'll have to come back here though - it'll go again because it's been out for so long"*. Anyway I used to have to go back about once a month or 6 weeks or something like that but he actually got me riding again.

In fact I even went hunting again, which I never thought I would do. But after all that time, my nerve had gone to start with, until I rode Hypy and got back into things again. So that was a bit of a problem for a while, but it all came back eventually. I still get backache though and it does pop out occasionally and so I go to an osteopath, and get it put back.

I thought Ronnie Longford had retired a long time ago, although recently I've heard that he might still be practising...

So, I thought, perhaps I can get back onto the farm full time now! And that's what happened.

Judy the Alsatian greets a friend from the Service in her MG when she came to visit after I'd finished working at the RRE

Chapter 7

A NEW ERA

A Happy Return

After I had resigned from the Service, I threw myself into the farm – I was back in my element full time again at last! However, I had made some good friends in the Service, some of who stayed close afterwards, especially Anne and Rosie. Anne went back to Ireland eventually, but Rosie is still here!

Joan and I still had a small dairy herd and a few horses, but we looked to expanding a little, now that I was back properly.

However, we also had some time for holidays for once, and we really enjoyed them.

*Jo on her
Fergie Grey*

Fishing

It was about then I did a bit of fishing for a time, fresh water and a bit out at sea on occasion - but certainly I was on my own for that as Joan really didn't like boats – she used to go green at the mere thought of it!

I went fishing with Colin, Joan's brother, when he lived at Rotherwas, near Hereford. We fished on the river Wye and the Teme too. We did some fly fishing too and Colin gave me one of the rods he had made from an aircraft radio aerial, by tidying them up and whipping the eyes on. He also made some really beautiful flies, copying the shape and colours of the mayfly. However, I think that Colin enjoyed making the equipment more than actually using it, and I carried on fishing long after he had gone onto other things.

Jo fishing on the River Teme
August 1961

I can remember going down to the river to do a bit of fly-fishing one day in May, with Joan and Laddie & Angela, and we were fortunate enough to see the hatch of the mayfly. That is one of nature's spectacles if ever there was one. It really is an extraordinary sight and I was absolutely spellbound and stood there watching it for a long, long time. Joan was with me and we just stood there watching it, entranced. There must have been millions of these little grey and white flies fluttering in all directions, a fantastic sight – it was difficult to believe such beautiful little things were to live for only a few hours or a day or so.

Jo contemplating a bit of sea fishing at Aldburgh, in 1982

Photo probably taken by Joan, at a distance.....

60

Later I went fishing in Wales quite a bit, usually with June and Margaret. But then one year we went up to Scotland. We stayed near Loch Awe and went round some little islands in a rowing boat called '*Summer Wine*' – this was in the early days of the TV programme involving Compo, Clegg and Foggy, but they didn't come with us and Joan stayed on shore with the dogs of course.

Joan, safely ashore, took this photo of a very cheerful Jo who was about to go hunting mackerel.

The boat was crewed by just a couple of local lads – they couldn't have been more than 13 or 14 years old – but they certainly knew what they were doing and could handle the boat as well as anyone. Well, the sea was flat calm, like a millpond it was, and they rowed us out to where they said our best chance was of catching a few mackerel. And we did!

Then they took us to a small, uninhabited island for a break and to have our packed lunches. Well, uninhabited it was, apart from some feral goats up on a ridge, together with a row of birds all looking down at us: a bunch of uninvited guests…..
It really was a lovely, relaxing and peaceful day.
One of those days you never forget.

A Boat Of Our Own

When I was gun-dog training, I met up with June once more, a friend I had known from carpentry classes some years before. We stayed in touch and once I had retired we enjoyed owning a small boat on the river for a time.

The 17 foot cabin cruiser, called 'Sunbeam', was share-owned by me and my friends June and Margaret. This allowed us to spend days on the River Avon as we moored the boat at Bredon. It was lovely on the boat because you saw at close hand the reed warblers, grebes, ducks with their babies - and the swans that were so majestic. They would come alongside the boat with their cygnets to take a look at us.

We were lucky enough one day to see a kingfisher about three metres ahead of us. We slowed right down and it flew ahead of us for quite some time, landing occasionally on overhanging branches.

On another occasion I remember that the chain that drove the propeller came adrift and guess who had to climb on the back of the boat – Jo Muggins! It was a bit hairy as we were getting quite close to the weir so I had to work fast. Whilst trying to climb back down into the boat I slipped and my right leg and right arm were right down in the water and we were all laughing so much I couldn't get myself back on board. Eventually the others helped me back on and all was well, if a bit wet.

The down side of owning the boat was the fact that every autumn we had to get it right out of the water and clean the whole of its bottom. A filthy job and no fun at all.

Sunbeam's Crew: Jo, Margaret and June.   But which one was the Captain?   1984

For a couple of years we stored it through the winter in the barn, where nowadays the pots and ornaments are kept for the nursery, but then we found we weren't really using it so we sold it.

Bird Watching

Then I also used to go bird watching. I've always been interested in birds and I had some very nice trips. One was up to the Farne Islands but Joan didn't come on these, she wasn't really that interested. She liked birds, but she wasn't all that keen on watching them - she just liked seeing them in the garden. So I went with two friends, John and Barbara, and it was a magical day, absolutely magic. It was a beautiful sunny day and all these birds were there with their babies. They landed us on Inner Farne and then took us to one of the other islands where you get dive bombed by the terns – you really do, so you have to put a hat on - and there are baby tern chicks all around your feet. You only walk along paths – you do have to stick strictly to the paths. And then on one path, right at my feet, was an eider duck 'sitting'. She never moved and I looked down at her and she looked up at me with a beady eye as much as to say *"Don't you dare.....!"* That's how 'tame' they were, it's wonderful really.

We also went down to Norfolk, we went to Titchwell and places like that. We went to Welney to see the floodlit feeds. Now that's a wonderful sight to see <u>all</u> those swans coming in, it's fantastic. How they all land and don't hit each other and collide I just don't know, it's another miracle.

An Amusing Side Show

I was good friends with Charlie Williams for many years and knew him to be a straight chap with no side to him, while at the same time being a 'good businessman'. At his place, that he called 'Archers Stud' for some reason, he traded in scrap and in just about anything else that came his way, and then spent his time and money on others too.

For example, every year he'd prepare his very fine Shires and their dray, all dressed up in their finery, and then he and his wife Do would take them to the Show for display and to take the children for rides, which they just loved - and called him *The Horse Man*.

(Also see Appx. 2&3)

Charlie's Shires on display (Charlie is the second in line)   Press photo

Anyway, on one occasion he got a good offer of some big barrels of oil and stored them in his yard. However, a young police officer, who they called 'Bev Cat' or something, got to hear about this and accused him of receiving stolen goods!

The police took him to court so he engaged Mr. Mott to defend him, who assembled witnesses to vouch for Charlie's good character – and they asked me too. I was happy to do this and spoke up in court when my time came to do so.

An amusing bit of doggerel, 'The Horse Man', was passed around afterwards:

The Horse Man

by Watta Witness

To court we went, Charlie and Me
To see the Magistrates one, two, three.
They soon found Charlie was no clown,
For he'd elected to go before the Crown.

Some weeks later we were ready for the fray
But the coppers put it off till another day.
At last we got inside that court
With lots of witnesses, all well taught.

There was Joan, and Geoff, and Barry Key
All prepared for this little spree.
Some of the jury looked a bit rough,
But Charlie said they was "near enough..."

So in the box old Charlie squat
And left the talking to Mr. Mott.
Then in they called that bloody Cat
And he sure talked like a proper pratt!

Big lies Cat told, which did him no good
For we blew him to bits like a piece of wood.
Then in come Jim Luther to say his bit
But what he said was a load of shit.

Now Charlie let fly at this poor sod
I bet the jury thought "Oh my God!"
"You're lost for words!" he told this chap
As he gave his box a bloody good slap.

Now into the box they called old Mick
And he for sure pulled a trick!
Charlie by now had swelling veins
So in we sent old Geoff Caines.

Geoff said his bit - it wasn't a lot
But he was thanked by Mr. Mott.
Big Joan spoke well for our old guy
(For the life of me I can't think why.....!)

Charlie's hands weren't as soft as they thought was his head,
But dear old Charlie worked his case in bed.
Charlie said Wilson was a good little mon
But we was all glad when he was gone.

They never called Do, she didn't mind that,
She'd more fun with Luther and that was that:
How he cussed and how he sweared!
(Jim didn't care but the folks all stared.)

A trial costs a lot in that big place
That's why John Lee stopped the case.
"Enough is enough!" he cried in vain
And told the coppers "Don't do this again!"

He told old Charlie to select his friends....
(And advised him then to buy some hens).
Out we came with case disproven
Into the car and back to Malvern.

They phoned the result to tell Bev Cat
I suppose he thought that was that?
But up to Hindlip the coppers went -
Some were straight but others were bent.

Poor old Bev nearly got the chop
He should be hung in a butcher's shop.
In future Bev, don't take sides
Because our kids have now lost their rides.

Not even the dray will be at their Show
Because I don't think Charlie intends to go.
"Please Mr. Williams will you come?"
"You stuff your show right up your bum!"

It just goes to show they don't win 'em all
If you really know how to set out your stall.
It might have sent Charlie a bit grey
But he'll be around for many a day!

At Archer's Stud you'll find the old chap,
Twisting the buggers for their scrap.
Yes, he'll be there to sweat and toil,
So long as he only buys Duckhams Oil.

Getting Around A Bit

In the mid 1980s we did get around quite a bit, and I've told you about going out to the Farne Islands. Well, we went to Seahouses first, right on the east coast and a lovely little village it is too, a small town really, and that's where we caught the boat out to the islands. Joan didn't come, she didn't like boats at all, but it was really worth it, seeing all the wildlife that you can't see on the mainland. But of course we also took the opportunity to visit Lindisfarne while we were up there. That was really worth visiting, but in a very different way to the little islands. It's full of history, with a castle and the remains of a monastery, which is why it's called 'Holy Island' I suppose.

Wikipedia

A view of Lindisfarne from the mainland

It was interesting driving out there, because we had to wait for the right time of the tides to go over the causeway – and had to time it right going back too!

For with the flow and ebb, its style
Varies from continent to isle;
Dry shod o'er sands, twice every day,
The pilgrims to the shrine find way;
Twice every day the waves efface
Of staves and sandalled feet the trace.

Sir Walter Scott

Pilgrims' Way   Wikipedia

They said that over 100 people actually live on the island nowadays – no monks left though! Now that would be an interesting sort of life – apart from all us tourists of course….

And then later we went to Duntisbury, and to Warkworth Castle too, in the Spring of 1984.

Jo sitting in front of the castle,
with the dachs and their Range-Rover

On other holidays we visited Hadrian's Wall, Chesters, Lacock Abbey and many other places over the years. Joan always said that there's far more of Britain than can be seen in a lifetime, which is why she never had much desire to go abroad.

But I did.

Rosie and I went for a lovely holiday in Spain – a real break from English weather! This was while I was still in the Car Service, towards the end, and we really needed a break. We stayed in a pretty little village on the coast, Estarit on the Costa Brava. I gather it's all changed there quite a lot now, but it was really very nice and quiet when Rosie and I were there.

We did a lot of walking along the coast and visited the Greek and the Roman ruins – that was fascinating.

Photo by Rosie

We also did quite a lot of swimming in the sea – and the waters were so clear and lovely and warm – I'd never consider doing that around Britain!

And we also visited a small island by boat, although there wasn't much to see there, but it was fun.

Gosh, that holiday was a real change for us – although we knew we'd then have to go back to driving cars around England......

Then, after I'd left the Service, I went to France with Pam for a week. We popped across the Channel to Normandy - and of course we went to see the island of Mont Saint-Michel. Amazing.

But – oh, how many steps up and down? I lost count very early on! It was all really worth seeing though, so wonderful and so much history – Joan would have loved it all I think, if only we could have got her out there!

Not now though – I couldn't face even the first flight of stairs!

Back At Home

There's no place like home, of course, and especially at Christmas. Joan and I always dressed the house up for Christmas, with holly and mistletoe and ivy here there and everywhere – and it was my job to go out and get it all, naturally. We also had, and I still have, some homemade decorations, including a model stable made from wood and cardboard, featuring Mary and Joseph and baby Jesus. It's nothing special, but it's always been an essential part of Christmas at Guarlford for us.

We were invited around for pre and post Christmas drinks each year, and usually with what seemed like a constant stream of visitors here too at that time – but we wouldn't have wanted it any other way. Then on Christmas Eve we would always go to the Midnight Service over the road at St.Mary's, where Joan had already decorated the church too! And then back for a nightcap before bed.

Christmas morning was busy because we always had a full, traditional Christmas Dinner with all the trimmings, so there was no time for looking under the tree to see if Santa had brought us anything…... unless we had family with us of course, in which case the children had to be catered for – not letting them open at least one present before dinner would have been a bit like cruelty to dumb animals!

Boxing Day usually saw the Hunt meeting locally, so we were out for all the morning, only getting back for lunch by the middle of the afternoon. But by then we'd usually been quite well lubricated and so were quite ready to tuck into some cold turkey. This was often with friends who had come back with us of course.

Photo by Donald

Boxing Day 1972 with Jo, Ruth, Joan and Rosie

More recently, without Joan, Christmas at home has been toned down a little, but in one way or another, friends still make it a good time – but I'll talk about it again later on.

69

It was a really severe winter in 1981. I can remember taking a few people, including Gordon Earp, and maybe Cath as well, up to Barnards Green to do their shopping when I went for mine as well.

Every day throughout that winter I had to go down to the bottom field to get the water running for the cattle. The tap was down in a small pit – filled with water. I had to roll my sleeve up and plunge down into there to turn the tap on. But of course the pipes were frozen, so I then had to make a small fire with straw and hay to thaw it all out, so we could get water into the water tank which, with a ball-valve, fed the trough for the cattle. I had to turn it off at night of course, and so it went, day after day throughout that awful winter. I wasn't just me of course, and Meriel Bennett remembers that hard winter too:

"We were all struggling to cope that winter and each day was long, arduous and stressful, but Jo didn't hesitate to offer lots of help to others."

Summer returned eventually, as it always has done so far, and then all the usual activities took place again, such as the annual Madresfield Show and its Marathon Drive for ponies and traps.

We used to go to the Show, but then drivers used to come to us too! Well, they passed our gate, anyway.

Chapter 8

RIDING TO HOUNDS

Now attend me, Diana and the Nymphs, for the lesson I would teach is one as to which even gods must differ and no two men will ever hold exactly the same opinion. Indeed, no lesson, no words, no lectures, be they ever so often repeated, will teach any man to ride to hounds. The art must come of nature and of experience.

Let it be understood that I am speaking of fox-hunting, and let the young beginner always remember that in hunting the fox a pack of hounds is needed.

Anthony Trollope, in the Pall Mall Gazette, 1865

All Of Jo's Horses....

Of course, dogs have been as much a part of my life as have horses. More so really, because I had a dog first and still have one now - but then horses are very intelligent and so they often have real character and can be closer in a way.

Robin   This was the first horse I knew that Joan owned.

Joan on Robin

I don't know where he came from but Joan bought him around about 1946 I think, because she told me she'd already hunted him hard for two years. I've already mentioned his racing prowess and a couple of his lightweight racing shoes are hanging on the wall here even today.

Carlisle Bay   Gaffer Tolley went to Leicester Horse Sales with Joan around 1949 and at about 3 o'clock in the afternoon Gaffer rang up to ask me to take the lorry up to Leicester as he'd bought a mare. Well, I went to pick her up. She was a lovely bay mare and we brought her home and tried her the next day. She turned out to be a lovely ride and had obviously been well schooled, so I hunted her in order to qualify her for point to pointing.

One unfortunate incident was when were going at a fair lick, on the flat, and she somersaulted and I went flying through the air, landed and broke my collarbone.

Her sad demise later was mentioned back in Chapter 4.

Conker This was an Irish Hunter who belonged to the Gaffer and myself and several friends of the Gaffer hunted him. One day Arthur Doorbar was hunting him and the Meet was delayed because of frost, so of course we'd all had a noggin or two. As four or five of us were jogging up the lane we saw four our five little paddocks each about two acres with cut and laid hedges and the temptation was too great so we all decided to jump them. We all went charging up and down over these hedges and suddenly Conker decided he'd had enough and he stopped dead at one of the hedges and Arthur shot over his head and landed face down on the top of the hedge, but his one foot was still in the stirrup. So Joan and I jumped off - we knew Conker - and we went slowly up to his head and he just stood there. The next job was to extricate Arthur's foot from the stirrup, which proved to be no easy job as we had to remove the stirrup leather. The episode rapidly sobered us up and we realised that if the Master had caught us we'd all have been sent home in disgrace.

Donegal This was Gaffer Tolley's show horse, so he was taken to all the shows in the hunter classes. He quite often won and was generally placed in the first three. Joan sometimes rode him and once in the Show Ring a loudspeaker blasted out right above his head and he went over backwards with Joan on board. She was very lucky not to be badly injured.
One day I rode him over the fences myself to give somebody a lead and he really was a lovely ride.

That was the end of our involvement with horses at the Gaffer's.

The Bay Filly In the early 1950s we bought a filly when she was three years old - but I can't for the life of me remember her real name. We broke her in and she really was quite beautiful, a lovely dark bay filly.
Our vet, who was Les Harries at the time, wanted us to put her into training with Fred Rimel to run in hurdle races, but we couldn't possibly afford it. Anyway, somebody must have heard about her because a man rang us up and said could he come and have a look at her? So he and his wife came to see her. They were lovely people - he was from Kenya, but they'd bolted because of the Mau Mau. He'd farmed out there and bred and sold polo ponies. He wanted to start doing it here and so he wanted her to ride and breed from. They liked her, he rode her and they thought she was lovely - and so they bought her. They came in to have a cup of tea and a drink and paid for the mare on the spot, telling us all about their life in Kenya. He was having to go back to shoot his polo ponies because he couldn't get them over here – he couldn't transport them and he wouldn't leave them to the mercies of the Mau Mau. They were both also worried to death about what would happen to their grooms and servants…. I don't think they ever knew what happened to them. Anyway, we saw them once or twice more and went down to see them - they were nice people and I felt sorry for them because I think it absolutely broke their hearts. I mean what a thing to have to do!
That was another small episode in our lives, and rather a sad one really.

Burnt Sienna

Burtie was a lovely liver chestnut who came from Bob Rouse, a neighbouring farmer who used to do our haulage, but also had an eye for a horse. Periodically we'd see his lorry come in and he'd often say *"I've got a horse, can you do something with it……?"*

Anyway, one day he came in and this time he had something rather special.

"I've got this horse and it's rather nice – you really should take a look at him….." We took a look and 'ummed' over it for a bit. He was called Burnt Sienna really, but we called him Burtie.

Anyway, Burtie really was something special. When a horse is very well behaved you say he's a perfect gentleman. Well Burtie was, right from the word go he wanted to please you and he was just lovely and we got so fond of him. We broke him in and he was so easy and really easy to break, he had a lovely temperament. We had him for a couple of years, because Bob would get these horses and we would break them in for him and get them going and hunt them or something like that. And then he'd sell them. This was something we just had to accept, but Burtie we'd got very fond of.

Inevitably the day came when Bob rang us up to tell us that he was bringing some people over.

"I think I've sold Burtie. There's some people from up north with a daughter at St. James' School in Malvern and they want to come down and see him." So on the Sunday morning they duly arrived. They were pleasant people with a very nice daughter called Sarah. She rode Burtie round the field and then we went out with her onto the roads. We took them for about an hour and then she went back into the field and popped him over a fence or two. He behaved as he always did, and so they bought him on the spot. We were a bit devastated really, but then they asked whether we could keep him for them! While Sarah was at the boarding school, they'd bring her down once a fortnight to ride Burtie. So we said yes of course we would and we were so pleased that we could have Burtie for another two or three years. And that's how it turned out, we kept him here at livery for their daughter for two more years.

Then of course, eventually the time came when Sarah left school and returned home and obviously she wanted Burtie home with her too, so we had to 'dispatch' him up to Yorkshire. This involved booking a railway wagon and we had to take Bertie up to Malvern Link Station's Goods Yard. They didn't use horseboxes on the railways so much in those days, it was only racehorse trainers that used proper horseboxes. However, the wagon was all ready for him and it was absolutely fantastic, knee deep in straw, fully padded all the way round and so it was impossible for him to hurt himself – it was a proper carriage for him, no expense spared. We put his hay in the corner and there was water laid on too. One of the railway men helped us put the ramp up and when he saw the inside of the wagon he loaded up into it with no fuss – he was such a good horse. So there he was, quite happy, all bandaged and rugged. But then Joan and I just fled. We got about 20 or 30 yards away before he neighed and neighed and neighed. I think the tears were falling for us too - it's so silly to get so fond of them, but you can't help it. So we took the dogs for a walk up on Midsummer Hill.

Sarah wrote to us regularly and sent us photos of Burtie, which was really nice of her. Then she got married and had a family and we simply lost touch after that I'm sad to say.

Cloudy Island

We had Angela Pearson-Gregory's thorough-bred mare called Hare Island and she was in foal to a stallion called Little Cloud, a fashionable sire of eventers at the time, being due to foal in May 1968. We got up early that day because we thought she'd foal early in the morning, in the front paddock, where the Nursery is now. It was about 6 o'clock on a beautiful May morning when John Barnett, who was a friend of ours and who had a stud over at Colwall, arrived. He knew the mare was due and so he came over to see that everything was all right - and then this beautiful foal was born. We called him Cloudy Island.

"Wow Joan, you've got something there!" he said and we really thought we had. Cloudy was a big, dark bay colt foal and was up on his feet and suckling in no time at all.

We thought *'My word! - Cheltenham here we come!'* Such are dreams are made of, I suppose. Anyway, he grew and he grew. But then he grew some more…. He got far too big - you want something about 16 or 16.1 hands, but this blighter grew up to 17 hands!

Unsurprisingly we had all sorts of trouble with him - and then his wind went. I met John Chugg in the Chemists and he said, *"How's that big horse of yours? Have you cut his throat yet?"* Everybody in there looked at us – what sort of people <u>are</u> they? they must have thought!

You see, very big horses are short of wind and you have to have an operation done which entails an operation on the windpipe, so that's what we had to get done.

When he was four we sent him to John Hagley to be broken in because at the time we were too busy to do it ourselves. He came back from John's, but Joan wouldn't ride him as he was too big for her, so I rode him, but he was down right wicked and tried to get you off - he didn't care if he hurt himself! One day when we were riding up the lane, a dog ran out, which usually snapped at the horses' heels. This time however, it jumped up at Cloudy's nose. He shot backwards and I went 'out the front door'! He was extremely active for a big horse - thoroughly naughty in fact - and I managed to concuss myself, gaining a lump the size of a goose egg on the back of my head. Joan was with me and we went back home and put him in the stables, but my head really was hurting by this time.

"I'd better take you to the doctor" said Joan. The doctor took one look and said that he wasn't touching me and that I should go straight to hospital. So Joan took me into Worcester. It was the old Worcester Infirmary in those days. So they X-rayed me and then I went back out and sat in the corridor waiting for the doctor with Joan. They eventually called me in and when I went in, Joan heard them say *"It's a fracture, definitely a fracture….."* So she went shooting into where the two doctors were looking at an X-ray - and it was obviously an arm! (There was a lady sitting out in the corridor with her arm in a sling.) So Joan sorted them out:

"It's Miss Newell – and it's her <u>head</u>, you idiots," Oh my God - utter consternation. Anyway, they then found my X-rays and got sorted. So, it seems that, but for Joan's intervention, I nearly had my arm put in a sling and the old lady would have had her head looked at.

They put me in a cubicle and said I'd got to stay in overnight. Joan had to take all my clothes home and they put one of these short shifts on me - and I was frozen stiff. (I often wonder how many patients they killed off, to be honest.) I lay there, shivering, and then a nurse came in.

"You can go home now."

"But – I was told I had to stay overnight! And I've got no clothes now – I'll have to stay."

"No. Go home" she said. Well, I thought *'What am I going to do?'* I knew that, as it was about half past six, Joan would be out feeding the horses, and the cattle, and going round the sheep, and no way would she hear the phone…. So I thought that I'd better ring Joan's cousin

Pam, who lived at Cradley - and hope that she was there. I did get hold of Pam and briefly explained what had happened.

"I'm in Worcester Infirmary and need to get home, so can you please go home and get me some shoes, a pair of trousers and a shirt and a bra and a pair of pants, and come and get me?" I said. *"You'll have to find Joan - she'll be around the buildings somewhere."* So Pam went and found Joan and duly turned up with my clobber and I got dressed and home I came. But I have no doubt in my mind that they shouldn't have sent me home. I felt very ill for several days afterwards and thinking back now, having had it happen again, I know that I was seriously concussed - but I think the sister wanted the bed.

Anyway, Cloudy was seen by Jack Gittings, who was a hunter judge and exhibitor, who put the word about and as a result we sold a half share in him to Sheila Wilcox who was going to show him. However, he still turned out to be very difficult and so he was then sold to David Tatlow and then to someone in Germany.

I've no idea what happened to him after that, but I'll talk about him again later.

Jo and Cloudy

Bertie
A good friend of ours was Molly Horton, from Crowle, whom we got to know years ago through selling her a horse. She later had a mare which her son, Peter, evented for a time. The mare was called Just Coral and she had a foal, which was called Bertie, a very different horse to Bob's horse Burtie from ten years earlier.

When Bertie grew, Peter evented him a couple of times, but then Peter had to go off and earn a living and so she got a girl in, called Michelle, to ride Bertie. She rode the horse for some time and we had a lot of fun doing that. Joan and I were the back-up team, we used to go and get the numbers and report on the event when Molly couldn't bear to watch. Bertie was a terrific horse and frightened Molly to death – sometimes she just couldn't look when they were competing. Joan and I had to report how he was going, but he survived all right.

We went all over the place. We went down to Windsor with the horse and he went very, very well there. Then we went to some place up in North Wales that really was quite a course - but they survived that all right too. I can't remember the name now. We did stay the night in a very nice pub that time, I do remember that. Really Bertie did quite well and we had a lot of fun. We also took him to Chepstow when they had an event there, which I think they still have, and Bertie was about 20 minutes off starting when he cast a shoe, so Joan and I had to go haring around to find the blacksmith. There's always a blacksmith on site at these events – a blacksmith and a vet – all the essential people. We collared the blacksmith and he came flying up and put Bertie's shoe back on, and away went Bertie. That was an interesting place to go to because it was held on the racecourse which is a beautiful spot. We'd been to the races there many times but we'd never been eventing there before. After that we went quite a few times.

All in all it was great, until eventually Bertie retired and that was the end of that for us.

Glory-Be, Charlie Fox & May-Be

We bought a foal from Charlie Williams, but it had never been handled at all even though she was about 8 months old. She was a liver chestnut and we called her Glory-Be because her mother was called Glory, but I can't remember the father's name. So Charlie led Glory down with the foal following behind, loose, at about 6 in the morning. We got them into a loose box and then he got the mare out again and well, you can imagine how it was then - the mare squealed and the foal squealed..... Anyway, he took the mare away and the foal went on shrieking all day until we eventually went into it. It was quite good tempered really, it wasn't nasty or anything, but just frightened to death I think. We nattered away to it and gave it some food and eventually it calmed down and turned out to be an absolute pet in the end. She simply loved people and used to follow us around like a dog. If she was out in the field and she heard us in the garden, she'd come up to the fence and neigh. We always had to go and say hello and give her a tit-bit of some sort, polo mints as a rule.

While we had to clean her stable out, we'd open her door and she would just walk up and down the yard for a bit until we called her back and then she'd amble back in again. One day we were doing this, and I was in the barn getting a bale of hay out, she came ambling down the yard and past the barn....

"And where do you think you're going?" I asked her, but she just walked up to the gate - and she just jumped it from a stand still! I couldn't believe it - you know how high it is, our front gate into the nursery. I fled down the drive, expecting to see her galloping off down the road, but no, not a bit of it. She just stood there and looked back at me, so I went out and got hold of her mane and led her back in.

"You silly old fool, frightening me to death like that!" I said to her, but she just looked at me, gave me a nudge, and ambled back up into her stable.

We broke her in at three years of age and then turned her away until she was four when she came into serious work. The only snag with her was that we were unable to hunt her, because the minute she saw the hounds she broke into a sweat and it poured off her like a tap. She was white lather from head to foot and she shook like a jelly. We kept that horse for many, many years.

She had a big colt foal who was born in the early hours out in the field on 27th April 1972, when just then we saw a fox run across the field. So as he was by 'Lord Fox', we called him 'Charlie Fox'. We showed Charlie Fox, and we even had a 'First' with the mare and the foal at Bosbury Show. But showing isn't our line of country really, we used to get bored to death, so we didn't do much more of that, but we were quite pleased for her sake really because she looked a picture that morning. Cath Lockley can remember it too:

"Oh yes, we took her to Bosbury - Mac came with me and Joan followed on in the car – and we got a First with the mare and her foal! But then my brother Roger and me were always across here helping the two Joans with whatever animals were around. Probably we were more of a hindrance than a help though....."

The next year, on May 4th, Glory had a filly foal, and we were lucky that foal lived because we didn't think she was going to foal until the morning. Being born in May, to Glory-Be, and her future seeming doubtful, we called her May-Be. Anyway, I'd popped out in the evening to see somebody or other and I came back and I thought that I'd better just have a look at the mare.... and it was a good job I did because she'd foaled and the foal was still in the sac in the corner of the box. So I had to get in there a bit quick and get it out and rub it down. Anyway, it was OK. It staggered to its feet and wandered round to where the milk was and started to suckle. I went and fetched Joan and when we got back they were well away. That's another of nature's miracles – how these animals know what to do and where to go. They manage it much better than we do.

Cath remembers showing all three of them soon afterwards.

"I can remember going to Madresfield Show with the mare and her two foals: Glory-Be, Charlie Fox and May-Be. I led 'em into the ring and we got a First with the colt, and then a Second with the mare and her filly foal. We were so proud of them!"

Jo with mare and foal in the back paddock

However, early one night when she was 12years old, Glory was very ill and so we sent for the vet, and he came pronto.

"Ah, she's got colic" he said. *"I'll dose her and then you'll have to walk her about a bit. But don't let her lie down."* You mustn't let them lie down because if they do they can roll and twist their gut.

However, she got worse and we rang him up again - and Charlie Williams too, bless his heart, he came down as well because we'd rung him up to give us a hand because it was a hell of a job keeping her on her feet. She wanted to lie down all the time. The three of us stopped out there and the vet kept coming back. (He was at a christening party for his new baby, so it was very good of him to keep coming back.) The vet came back several times and injected her to stop the pain, but we were making no progress.

"I'll give her one more dose and come back in an hour's time" and this is what he did, but then he finally came back just once more…..

"Well, I'm afraid that she's obviously got real damage of some sort inside there…. I'm really sorry, there's nothing for it, but to put her down." So at about 11.30pm we had to put her down.

He said to leave the foal with her overnight, so we did and when we got up in the morning and went out, there was the foal still lying by the dead mare. I can tell you Joan and I had a weep or two….. And what to do with the foal?

In those days the kennels took any dead stock off the farm and so they were coming the very next morning. But Charlie had turned up already and he took charge.

"You two go off down the field with foal…off you go now, bugger off…." That was Charlie's way of saying things. So of course we did. We took May-Be down the field and fed it and made a fuss of it and when we got back up the mare had gone. The box was cleaned out, knee deep in straw, water and hay in there for the foal. Charlie knew what to do. He was a very good friend to us I have to say.

That's one of the downs, but that mare had given us a lot of joy over the years and you get the highs and the lows……but that's keeping horses.

May-Be was only just four months old when her mother died, so she was turned out with Joan's horse Billy, who turned out to be a real old 'Granny' to her. When she was about four years old she went to Robert Oliver to be shown as she was very pretty, but later he sold her to a girl who had seen her and liked her.

Boffin   He was an ex-eventer who was loaned to Rosie and we all thought he was going to be a super ride, but instead of which he just leant on the bit with a completely dead mouth and all the weight was on your hands. No fun at all. Later he became lame and his owner had him back.

Timmy   Strangely, Timmy and Billy came from the same stables. The trainer rang us up and asked us if we would take him, as he couldn't jump and therefore couldn't be raced. However, he was a lovely ride, being a pretty dark bay, at about 16 hands. Joan rode him mostly as he wasn't too big – but it was true - he couldn't even jump a twig. We tried all the dodges, but Timmy just didn't want to know…..

    But, I just can't bring myself to tell how Timmy died, even after all this time…..

Billy   We went to see another horse at the trainer's up on Bredon Hill in 1972. The horse was called Billionaire, although known always as Billy, being a big, dark bay, almost black, and according to Joan's diary entry on 30th August he was '*lop eared and amiable*'.

    He had run in The Derby, coming fifth, but really he was too big at 16.3 hands to race that young and he was gangly too. The trainer then had him trained to go in The Champion Hurdle and they really fancied his chances there, but they wanted to give him a hurdle race beforehand. So they picked out a race for him to run in, but the day before the race the trainer found heat in his leg. If you have heat in a horse's leg you don't run him, you just don't, because it's almost 99% sure you're going to break him down, which means the tendon goes. So he told the owner that he shouldn't run, but the owner insisted that he did run. They had a bit of to-do over it I think, but the owner pays the bills and so he had his way and sure enough, they broke him down. So it finished his racing days really - it was a bad break down, he had a bowed tendon. In the end I think his only real claim to fame was that he'd carried the favourite out at Tattenham Corner. However, the owner then said: "*We'll find him a good home…..*"

    It was the trainer that had rung us up and when we saw Billy we sort of fell in love with him - a great big gangly soft thing he was.

    So we agreed to give him a good home and hunt and hack about on him.

    Joan was especially fond of him, although really he was too big for Joan, but she got on with him all right. He was a gentle giant really and we took him here and we took him there, and he went hunting too.

    Joan had a lot of fun with him, we did a bit of this and a bit of that and bit of the other and he stayed sound for many years. Mind you, we looked after him, saw his legs were bandaged after he'd been working or anything, we did care for him.

    He lived with us until he was about 30 odd and he's buried in the field at the back of the house.

Joan on Billy

Hypy   She was really called Hyperbole and was about ten or eleven when she was bought by Rosie.

Hypy had really come to the end of her point-to-point days and wanted a good home. Rosie, myself and Joan all hunted her but she was always regarded as being Rosie's horse – to such an extent that in August 1973 she attended Rosie's wedding to Donald McCarry.

From left to right:
Rosie, Hypy, Donald

Norman May Studios

79

Rosie enjoyed riding Hypy with us and we all used to go to events together at times. She recalls one particularly memorable adventure:

"On one occasion, the three of us, the two Joans and myself and the two horses, Hypy and Timmy, went all the way up to Rutland for a week's riding/trekking holiday. We set off knowing it was going to be a long journey, especially towing a trailer. Unfortunately, going up a steep hill, the car suddenly decided to conk out! So there we were completely stuck, 'till a good Samaritan came by and helped Jo fix it.

The establishment we went to was all very grand, with lovely stables for the horses and super accommodation for us in the house. We were given jumping lessons in the indoor school, dressage instruction and were then sent off round the cross-country course, which was very exciting. I ended up sailing over Hypy's head at one of the jumps! It was a hole in a thick high dark hedge, which Hypy didn't like, so she stopped dead and on I went bridle in hand! She just stood there waiting for me to get up and get going again.

On the last evening we were all invited to drinks with the teacher and her husband, Colonel Sturrock. It was very formal, with us all in our skirts and blouses, trying to look and behave elegantly! It was a good holiday and we all enjoyed it very much."

There's a good picture later on in this chapter of Rosie on Hypy and me on Jakey taking part in the Long Distance Ride.

Jakey   Because of my back injury, I had been without a horse and hadn't even ridden for some time, but at last my back was much better and I was sort of thinking about getting a horse again when a friend of ours, Verity Pease, said that she knew of an ex-chaser who was in need of a good home where he would be hunted, and would I have him? So Jakey duly came into my life.

When I had him he was not in top condition, but we took him in and had the vet worm him and we fed him and eventually he began to get into being quite a handsome fellow.

He soon improved, got stronger and I rode him about quietly at first and without doubt he was the most comfortable horse I had ever been on. This was very fortunate because, after being out of the saddle for so long, my nerve had gone a bit, but Jakey looked after me.

One day I was out with Rosie and Joan and I was ahead of them up Wood Street. Now, I grew to know that he had funny little turns and he'd dance about a bit and canter sideways, and jump up and down and do little half-rears – nothing too rough. But Joan and Rosie looked at each other and said: *"That's done it - she'll never get on him again....."* but it didn't worry me! I just laughed at him because he wasn't trying to get me off, there was nothing nasty in it, it was just high spirits, that's how he was. Jakey and I had great fun together.

As he got stronger we went hunting which he loved - he was a fantastic jumper, having chased of course, and I had some fantastic days out with him and he simply loved to be up with hounds.

We also did a bit of cross-country, show jumping and even dressage which Jakey thought was a complete and utter waste of time. I was persuaded to take part in a dressage test, "*You'll do well,*" they said, "*because he moves so well.*" I was told that the arena would be marked in sawdust so I practiced on sawdust to get him used to it. However, when we arrived to do the test, the arena was marked out in something shiny and black. Jakey took one look at it and said to me '*You must be joking!*'

To say we made an entrance! – well, we did a passage where we should have walked, we did some beautiful movements, but sadly not where and when we should have done. Every time I looked at the judges they were killing themselves laughing, they thought it was hilarious.

At the end they gave us a 'critique' and they said, "*A beautiful horse, but you both need more practice.*" Without a doubt, hunting was Jakey's great joy.

Hunting

*Jo on Jakey
at The Swan, Newland*

*Jo at a Meet at Hanley Swan
in the 1960s*

*Another Meet at Hanley Swan,
20 years later*

Rosie and Jo

*Rosie on Hypy and Jo on Jakey,
with the Croome Hunt,
at The Bush at Callow End .....*

Press photo

..... and Jo back from hunting.

Rosie and I also took part in a Long Distance Ride in the Forest of Dean, which was really good fun, with good weather, company and drinks!

Jo on Jakey and Rosie on Hypy in the Forest of Dean   Press photo

We even attempted to take part in a Musical Ride at Madresfield, but as Rosie recounts this wasn't Jakey's cup of tea either:

"Either in 1971 or 1972, The Avenue Riding School was asked to do a Musical Ride at the Madresfield Show in August. So Jo and I went along to have a go. I went with Hypy and Jo was on Jakey. Unfortunately Jakey took exception to The Keel Row blaring out through the loudspeakers. He very nearly turned himself inside out! He wouldn't stay still for a minute. So Jo had to ride Fred, one of Avenue Riding School's horses instead! Needless to say Jo wasn't at all happy with this..... Hypy was perfectly well behaved though and we really enjoyed ourselves. Hypy and I, if not Jakey and Jo, thought 'The Ride' was a great success on the day, congratulations all round!"

*Rosie on Hypy just before the Musical Ride
and behind them is Jo on Fred, the horse borrowed from the School
(Lancia Flavia parked behind)*

Cath remembers it too:

"It really was a hoot, Jo having to leave Jakey and ride Fred instead! I didn't take part at that one, because the children were little and I wasn't riding then.

But we often went to various point-to-points too: Ledbury, at Bushley and the Heythrop, at Fox Farm. I suppose my Mum and Dad went more often than I did though. I do remember going to the Upton point-to-point and we took a picnic in the back of the cars and we all sat up on the bank to watch. We, that's me and my brother Roger, we helped when we could."

"On another occasion" remembers Rosie, *" Jo and I were riding over the Old Hills and came to a small gate out of a field. Well, no way would Jakey stand still for Jo to open the gate, so I had to get off Hypy and oblige. Jakey was making such a fuss about getting through the gateway that Hypy got fed up with waiting there on her own and set off up the hill towards home. I had to run after her in my clumsy riding boots shouting, 'Wait Hypy! Come back here!' In the end I caught up with her and all was well, but it's just another 'Jakey Episode' that we remember!"*

Jo on Jakey

A commissioned oil painting by Robert Bartleet

They say that in your life there's one dog, one horse, one man or woman, as the case may be, and he was my one horse.

Jakey was very good for my ego, because Joan wouldn't get on him after he'd cantered all the way up the main road with her – sideways - and she couldn't stop him! Rosie just wouldn't ride him at all. But he was very good for me - we just clicked and we got on. You do, sometime, with some horses.

I was heartbroken when he died, but there you are.

Remembering Miss Whicker

In amongst all this business with the horses another character we got to know was a lady called Miss Whicker, who was a really wonderful lady. She belonged to a family who owned Woollas Hall on Bredon Hill, but in some financial crash they lost all their money. She'd become a teacher when we got to know her.

She had a horse, an Arab stallion called Tackamir, and she used to ride him all over Bredon Hill. She would sometimes have this stallion at stud, so she'd take him to where she had the visiting mares in a field separately away from the house. I don't suppose you've had anything to do with a stallion, but it's all very violent. The stallion stamps and chucks his head about roars and snorts and blows. It's all quite alarming really, but she said that he was as good as gold....

Now, when you bring the stallion to the mares, the mares show whether they are ready for service or not. If they stand with their tail up, you can see quite obviously that they're ready. So then she'd take him back to the stable by herself – this was a very little old lady, she wasn't as big as Joan and she was quite old, must have been about 60 - and she'd put his stallion head-collar on and take him back to these mares one at a time. Usually a man would come and help her, but she used to hold the stallion herself - and he became a different animal when he'd got his stallion head-collar on. He knew what it was all about and he really roared and plunged and jumped, and well, behaved just like a stallion does. As I said it's a very violent business – but Miss Whicker coped with it all.

She was ill at one time and she asked if I would go over and walk him for her. So I went over and walked this stallion up and down the road to give him some exercise - and I can tell you, he was a right old handful. Mind you I was fairly young and fit then, but he ran at me and wore me out. I mean, he walked like a train. Just how she had managed him I really don't know. I was trotting to keep up....

Eventually of course, Tackamir died and Miss Whicker was heartbroken, poor old soul. She was an extraordinary lady, always cheerful, you wouldn't think she had anything to worry her although she'd had a lot of upsets in her life, what with her family and the Hall and everything. So she was a lady worth remembering.

Throughout the time in the world I've lived in, there's been so many interesting, lovely, memorable people and animals – I've been so very lucky.

Admiral Benbow, in Grange Farm's stables
1961

Shiela Wilcox and Her Horses

We met Shelia Wilcox through a horse we'd bred. In the early 1970s we had a stallion called Cloudy Island that I've already talked about and that we wanted rid of. We sent him to a chap called Jack Gittings who showed him. Jack did quite well with him in the showing ring, but then Sheila Willcox saw him and she said she might buy him. However, then she decided that she wouldn't.

"What do you think about a half share?" I asked her – anything's better than nothing, after all.

"Yes, O.K. we'll have a go." So that's how we got to know Sheila.

Just to finish off his story, Cloudy next demolished six huge flower tubs that were in front of the stables at Sheila's place, careered across the yard and fell into a ditch.... We decided that if Sheila and her head girl, Jeanette, couldn't handle him then nobody would be able to! So we sold him to David Tatlow who hunted him and then he was sold onto Germany, as I've told before.

I think the older ones will remember Sheila - she was a European Champion Event Rider in 1957 and again in 1959, when the team won Gold medals both times! Mind you, she started early, and rode in a Three Day Event with her horse, High&Mighty, when she was only 18. She also won Badminton for three consecutive years (1957, '58 & '59) and was the first woman rider in the UK to achieve international success. This was on her new mount, Airs&Graces – and I think that nobody since has ever won it three years running!

She'd had an awful accident in 1971, a fall at the Tidworth Horse Trials, which left her partially paralyzed, and that's how we first met her, but it hadn't slowed her down much it seemed and she was doing very well in dressage, on Son&Heir.

Sheila Wilcox
Press photo

As we got to know her better, Sheila asked us if we would be prepared to have her resting eventers and dressage horses at livery. We were flattered and pleased to do so, especially because it was a very useful added income for us. However, this was quite a responsibility because they were damned expensive, I can tell you. Some times we had two or three, sometimes we'd have half a dozen – and I shudder to think what they would all have added up to.....

So, we had those valuable horses of hers here and it was a bit of a nightmare for us both at times. You'd hear banging in the night and you'd think, *'Oh God! - I wonder if one's got cast'* and you'd go flying out in your pyjamas just to see, but they were always OK. It was really interesting having those lovely horses with us of course and we had all sorts of famous people from the horse world who would come here to see them.

We also went to Ascot Horse Sales with Sheila, which was very interesting and enjoyable too. So we had a lot of fun with Sheila's horses and we had a lot of fun with Sheila too, as we all got on very well. She gave us free tickets to go to here, there and everywhere, often for various shows and every year she leant us her pass for The Badminton Horse Trials. We also went to Goodwood to the Dressage Finals, not that dressage was quite our cup of tea, but it was interesting to go and see all the same.

By then I had left RRE and we were rearing calves for barley beef, so what with the horses and the calves we were getting on quite nicely for a while really. The calf rearing was something else of course. Not easy, as I used to have to go to market and buy week old calves, although we tried to buy as many privately as we could. One way and another we kept going.

When I think about it now, I think we were either very brave or very foolish, I don't know which – or just mad perhaps?

Mind you, we had help, not least from Cath, who helped wherever and whenever we needed it. I do hope she doesn't regret it:

"I can remember looking after some of the livery horses occasionally" says Cath. *"I also cleared the muck from the fields when Joan and Jo were on holiday and generally helped with jobs."*

I still have many memories of Sheila's horses: some of them were exported over to America and some of them went on to great things in the eventing or dressage worlds. There were so many of them – and I can't remember all their names, nor do I have photos of them, but memories of those good times are still with me.

Sonny
Son&Heir belonged to Sheila Wilcox and we had him here for his annual holiday. He was Sheila's dressage horse and she assured us that he <u>didn't</u> jump. However, one day Joan and I were doing some fencing out in the field, and Sonny was in his paddock, when all of a sudden I felt a nudge in my back and, lo and behold, there was Sonny looking at us! He had obviously jumped out of his paddock over the post and rails. So Arthur Beauchamp and I put an extra rail on the top. Apart from that incident he was a lovely horse to deal with.

The Sheik
We had Sheik for some weeks, and he was a lovely horse that Joan and I enjoyed having with us.

He was then bought from Sheila Wilcox by May-Anne Tanskey, who then sold him to Mike Plumb in the United States. With Mike he came second in the American Open Championship.

The Sheik taking tea with Joan

Sheila also made a film about her exploits. It was called *The Event Horse*, which was premiered in London in 1975 - and we were there!

It was based on Sheila's book of the same title and follows the training of a young novice horse to competition level.
It was directed by Robin Crane and the commentator was Michael Clayton who was well known for commentating at national events.

It was a fantastic 'do' with champagne and food that was out of this world. Well, very different from our world anyway!

Jo at the Reception for the Premier of The Event Horse *London, 1975*

Press photo

It was towards the end of the period of 5 or 6 years looking after Sheila's horses that we were thinking about alternative ventures and that's when we stopped farming altogether I suppose, and we started the Nursery.

90

... And All Of Jo's Dogs

Throughout my life I have had a succession of dogs, often more than one at a time and in fact, apart from the war years, I have never been without a dog – and don't want to be .

As a child we had an old English sheepdog called Bob who sadly was involved in a car accident and so he had to be put down. To take his place we had a cocker spaniel called Dash.

After the war I had a mongrel dog, I think I've told you, he had a bad case of 'wander lust' and it was impossible to keep him in! He had a habit of visiting one house in particular about four miles away and my poor father got fed up with having to go and fetch him home.

So I asked the people in the house if they'd like to keep him? They agreed and so that was the end of our troubles.

Judy   The first dog that Joan and I had at Grange Farm was Judy. We'd seen an advert for the puppies in the Malvern Gazette. She was a German Shepherd and turned out to be a lovely dog in every way – guard dog, companion and all round good company and we kept her until she died at the good age of twelve.

Whenever I was out, Judy would sit at the end of the barn and Joan always knew when I was coming home and about a mile away because Judy would get up and walk down to the gate. She obviously recognised the sound of my car even at that distance.

Judy had two litters and when Cath was a little girl she used to spend hours playing with Judy and the puppies – that big, fierce guard dog was very good with all the children.

91

Jo and Judy's first puppies

One day however, we had an incident with another dog. I was driving the tractor, with 4 or 5 kids and Judy on the trailer, when this dog came flying out of one of the houses trying to attack Judy. What to do? I just put my foot down and fled down the main road, going flat out instead of turning into the farm – I didn't dare stop! Eventually the dog tired and just sloped off home and so we turned round and arrived safely back at the farm.

On another occasion the police came and warned us that an escaped prisoner was on the loose in the area and that he was dangerous. They searched the buildings and then said that he might be hiding up in the barn, which was full of hay at the time. The policeman asked me to go up and take a look...

"No I bloody well won't!" I told him. *" I'm not going all the way up there just to get hit on the head by a man on the run – it's your job!"* So up he went, and all was clear.

At that time my parents were in their seventies and were living in Cedar Cottage and so I decided to leave Judy there as guard dog for the night. My Dad was concerned that she wouldn't settle, but she didn't bat an eyelid and was perfectly behaved all night.

Meg   Our vet turned up one morning with a sheep dog puppy which he put on the floor, whereupon it shot under the dresser and we didn't see it for the next few hours – this was Meg. When she got to know us she was a lovely little dog. The vet's dog had had puppies and his wife had had twins - and they were living in a flat in Worcester! So naturally he was anxious to get homes for the puppies a.s.a.p., so he landed this one on us. She turned out to be the best working dog anyone could hope to have. She was very quiet and got on well with all the children - they all loved Meg.

The most fantastic story concerning Meg is when one Christmas the local children were staging the nativity story in church and, lo and behold, as the shepherds processed down the aisle who should be following them but Meg.....! She always met the children from the school bus and used to walk up the lane with them and then come toddling back.

On one occasion a newcomer to the village complained to the police that a sheep dog was attacking the children.   A very nice policeman turned up and wanted to see this 'fierce dog', so we produced Meg and I explained how she met the children off the bus - even going to church with them at Christmas - and said that I could produce several mothers who would bear all this out.

The policeman said to just forget it as he could see that Meg was a very good dog.

She lived until she was nineteen and a half.

Meg & Judy,
with Opal & Glory in their stables

Sue

Our English Setter, Sue was a loveable, but thoroughly disobedient dog. We loved her, despite setters not really being our sort of dog.

Sadly she developed demodectic mange which in those days was incurable. Eventually the irritation was driving her mad and on the vet's advice we had her put down when she was only two years old.

It was very sad.

Sue and two foals behind the house

Sally

Sally was the second German shepherd that we had and we had her as a guard dog. One day we had some friends here for the night and they had parked their car up by the buildings. Half way thought the evening Peter, one of the friends, went to fetch something from the car. After a while we began to wonder where Peter was, so I went up to the buildings to see where he'd got to and I heard a little plaintive voice:

"Jo! Jo - your bloody dog's got me pinned down!" Peter was leaning back against the car and Sally was lying down a few yards from him. Every time Peter moved Sally growled and got her hackles up – so Peter wasn't going anywhere! I called Sally to me and all was well.

Jo doing some logging in the fields in October 1981, with Sally demanding attention, while Lisa looks on.

Jo has on her old army leather jerkin and using their first Series II swb Land-Rover.

94

The Pack of Dachs

Over the years we had a succession of miniature long haired dachshunds: Tansy, Katy, Tweedie and Honey.

Tansy

The first was Tansy, who I bought for Joan as a present for having cared for both sets of parents for so long. I collected Tansy on the Saturday morning, while Joan was staying with her brother Colin, and so she spent the first weekend with me. When Joan came home on the Sunday evening I hid Tansy in the other room and Joan came in and was standing in the sitting room. Well, as soon as I let Tansy in she went straight to Joan – completely ignoring me with whom she had spent the last 48 hours! Tansy never left Joan for the next sixteen and a half years.

She turned out to be the best 'ratter' we ever had and was real character. Her nickname was 'The Duchess' because she always trotted along with her head held high and her tail up and no other dog would ever go sniffing round her.

Katy

She was bought to keep Tansy company if we had to leave them at home. However we more than often used to land up taking them both out with us. Katy was much quieter and used to follow Tansy around like a kid sister. When Tansy died, Katy came into her own and became much more of a character in her own right.

Katy and Lisa on the lawn outside the house

Tweedie

Next in line came Tweedie, who was a lovely little dach, but not with quite the same amount of character as the others.

Honey

Dachshunds are really hunting dogs and on one occasion we lost Honey on Castlemorton Common when she set a rabbit up and went off after it hell for leather. For a while we really thought we had lost her but thankfully she eventually came back of her own accord.

Then we went to Hartpbury and Joan had got her little dachsie, called Honey, who for some unknown reason had a 'thing' about horses and when a horse went by she'd chase it. Ian Stark, who was quite a famous rider in those days, went past, and Honey took off after him. Fortunately, she was on the long extension line, but she went 'whhiiippp....' after this horse as he went by. My friend Molly said *"Oooh! - I do hope that line doesn't break......"* so Joan kept her up short after that.

We were on the Common with her several times and if horses came she just took off after them. My cousin Lyn had a riding school over on Castlemorton and one day she went past with a gang of riders and off went Honey, going flat out, ears flapping up and down and little legs going so fast you could hardly see them. Eventually she came back of course.

"I saw your little dog! I didn't know whether to stop or whether to go on" said Lyn.

"It's a good job you went on, because she'd have been all in amongst you and she'd probably have got herself kicked to death!" I told her.

So when we saw, or even heard horses, we had to put Honey on a line quick, because we could never stop her. She chose to go completely deaf. It was no good calling *"Honey!"* or blowing your whistle – you'd blow your teeth out first.

Joan on Glory,
Jo & Katy, Brian Walker, Tanzy & Rosie,
Sally

96

Gun Dogs

Lisa   When I gave up hunting because of my back problems and then lost my horse, Jakey, I thought that I really had to do something and so I got a gun dog, Lisa. We went gun-dog training and I met some very good friends there and had a lot of fun.

Lisa was a Munsterlander and it was at the gun dog classes where I met June again whom I had known in carpentry classes some years before. So that was how June, Margaret, Joan and I got friendly again.

June introduced me to Laddie Bishop who ran The Duckswich Shoot and he said that I could take Lisa along to the shoots. So for the next few years I had a lot of fun with Lisa and June and her dog, Tess.

June, and Jo with Lisa

We worked the dog on Laddie's shoot down at the other side of Upton at Duckswitch, and had a lot of fun there and I thoroughly enjoyed myself.

It was a small shoot and the guns and the beaters and the pickers-up all mucked in together, there was no 'them and us' we were all good friends and every year we used to have a Shoot Dinner. But then we used to have a lovely meal after almost every shoot which Angela, Laddie's girlfriend used to cook for us, and all in all we had a really good time there.

Laddie,
Jo and Lisa

Duckswitch Shoot

Lisa and I got on quite well with my new sport - and I even won a competition.

Ernie and Brian,
Jo and Lisa

Gundog Trials

Jo and Lisa at their Test

Cirencester Park Gun-Dog Skurry. Winners: Jo & Lisa   Press photo: Graham Cox

The Springers

Nell   She was the first of my 'Rescue Dogs' and she came from Wiltshire. Nell was three when she came to me and she had been badly mistreated by a large burly man. Ever after that she never lost her fear of unknown men - and for some reason she was also afraid of aluminium ladders. The first time the window cleaner came with his ladders she vanished and when he had gone I found her down in the field sitting up in the middle of the grass. The next time he came she sat on the stairs with me but she shook and shook and shook. Despite this she turned out to be a lovely dog, very affectionate.

A very strange thing happened one day with Nell, when a friend of ours came to see us with his family. This man, Frank, was seriously ill at the time, and despite Nell's fear of strangers, especially men, she almost instantly went and lay at his feet.

Nell lived until she was twelve.

100

Meg

Next in line came Meg who came to us at 18 months old because her previous owner's daughter turned out to be allergic to dogs.

She was the easiest dog you could ever have, you could take her anywhere and always be able to rely on her. We had her until she was twelve.

Meg
A commissioned painting by John Horton

Lucy

My current dog is the third of the Springers and my third rescue dog. Lucy arrived in January 2012.

She started off as a very nervous little dog, frightened if you raised your voice and cowering if she thought there was anything wrong. She was also car sick to start with, which was a real pain, but she's alright now, touch wood. She's obedient, not bad at all and always pleased to see me! Her tail wags her whole body, so she's been nicknamed 'Waggle'. She's got a lovely coat – much nicer than Meg's, which was really rough and shaggy.

Another good thing about her is that she'll come every time, and shows no desire to chase anything. Oh, I'll always put her on the lead if there's any sheep about, but it's quite possible that it's not needed – she's well trained. Apart from the fact that she's a thieving hound – I was going to give John a nice piece of quiche one lunchtime, but she got it first! It's her only fault I suppose, and anyway it was only John who missed out, not me.....

Jo and Lucy,
January 2012

Photo by John

Overall, and looking back, my best dog ever was Meg I suppose. You could take her anywhere and be sure she'd behave – I could take her to see the Queen and she wouldn't disgrace me. She'd always come to heel – although she seemed to think about it for a second or two first......

So here I am, at nearly 90 years old, – and I've still got a good dog at my feet.

Chapter 9
AN EXCITING VENTURE

From Beef to Trees

Our finances were not doing so well by the early 1970s. The herd of 25 or so Ayreshire cows had gone, so we were no longer producing any milk for sale, and instead we'd got about 70 Friesian barley-beef bull calves. We were seeing the Bank Manager rather more often than usual, when one day he dropped a bombshell on us.

"Get out of your barley-beef and don't buy any more calves, because the price of barley will rocket and your sort of farming is all going to collapse soon." Now this was a shock, because that's what we had done for the past twenty years and we loved it. However, he was a countryman from farming stock, so he knew what he was talking about, as he was a really good Bank Manager too. So we took him at his word and bought no more calves that year. He saved our bacon – if not our beef!

Sure enough, the barley-beef collapsed because the price of corn was shooting up. So we were thinking *'What on earth are we going to do……?'*

Now, between us and the road towards the Rhydd we had a good row of elm trees, but at around that time they were really suffering from elm disease. They all had to go and there we were, all bare and left wide open to the road. Joan's brother, Colin, was here one day and he had a suggestion.

"Why don't you buy a big batch of trees and shrubs to replace them – buy them wholesale and sell the surplus?" It seemed a good idea and we looked into it.

We were really surprised at what a good bargain it was to buy them in bulk and so, never doing things by halves, we jumped in with both feet. We bought lots of them, planted what we needed and with the rest we started a business. We'd gone to Wye Vale Nurseries, in Hereford, and met a chap who gave us all sorts of advice.

"Oh you want this, lots of that and some of the other……."
Well, we got carried away and that's how Grange Farm Nursery started.

It was the best thing we ever did. Little did we know at the time that it was the start of continuous growth, because it was just a big new venture for us, a gamble. But just look at what it's grown into nowadays – and right from the start we enjoyed doing it. And then we had a business to sell when we retired.

New beds along the path to the house, the area now used as a car-park

Grange Farm Nursery

We were starting from scratch, but learned as we went along. Joan knew more than I did, but we both went on day courses to Pershore Horticultural College a couple of times.

I'm not saying I didn't know anything, of course I did! I mean, my mother was a keen gardener and Joan's father was a very good gardener too, so we had both picked things up already. You don't realise it at the time, but all through your youth and so forth you pick up things, but you probably don't know what you've got between your ears until it comes in useful.

A view of the new nursery, looking towards the main gate, from across the garden gate

We sort of knew what we wanted to do, and what we didn't want. We didn't want all the extras - the concrete gnomes, water-features, restaurant and play-area that come with a 'garden centre' so that's why we called ourselves a 'nursery'.

The Nursery's very first Price List

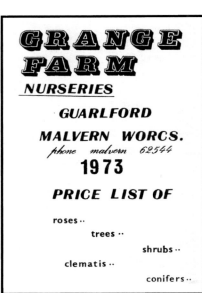

GRANGE FARM

NURSERIES

GUARLFORD

MALVERN WORCS.

phone   malvern 62544

1973

PRICE LIST OF

roses··

    trees ··

        shrubs··

clematis··

        conifers··

The barn was emptied completely to store new stock – and when I was building it back in the early 1950s I'd never even dreamed that it would be used for this!

The small paddock in front of the stables was cleared as well and used to display the plants and saplings and to make an inviting first view of the nursery for potential customers.

Mr.Beecham helped us with that, because he was a real old timer and a fount of knowledge who knew all about that sort of thing, having worked on the land – and for us – for many a long year. So Arthur dug the beds and sorted out all the drainage ready for the stock, which was good going for man of his years – he was well and truly retired by then, but he still lived just around the corner in Penny Close and was always happy to pop round and give us a hand.

After a couple of years we were getting along quite well, still with horses in the stables of course – we had other people's horses because we really enjoyed it. At times, this meant that Joan and I were really very rushed with all the new customers on top of all the usual jobs and the nursery too, but we got by.

Because we were established by then as a local business, we were asked by a local secondary school if we'd take on a young lad for three or four weeks on Work Experience, which was a new thing in those days. Happy to do anything to help, we agreed and the spotty youth arrived the following Monday morning. Well, he was a cheerful and pleasant young lad and he could make tea, but he wasn't any help to us for anything else at all so far as we could see because the poor lad suffered from an unfortunate allergy. He was allergic to work.

"You really are a lazy lump, aren't you?" I said to him before very long.

"Yes, I am really" he promptly replied, which took the wind out my sails a bit - I mean, how do you reply to that? We contacted his supervisor and she pulled him out.

Incidentally, she phoned us up a bit later to tell us that he'd since had a very successful work experience with the Council, where the road gang had found him to be very useful and he'd got on very well indeed. I said I wasn't surprised, as he was indeed good at making tea......

We wanted no more of those Work Experience time-wasters thank you very much, so when we were very quiet in the Nursery, in January or February 1975, and a young girl turned up out of the blue on her moped and asked if she could have a job, we told her *'no thank you'* - but we did take her telephone number. I am so glad that we did, because the 15 year-old was Carol Tozer.

Two of our very early customers, who really liked the new Nursery and frequently came to buy small items.

Photo taken behind the house, in the paddock.

Three Women in Business

We were really busy the following May and Joan and I were feeling in need of some help in the nursery, especially during the weekends when we got most customers, as is still the case. Enthusiastic young Carol must have made an impression on us because we dug out her phone number and thought about it again.

"We'd better ring that kid and see if she's still interested in coming" I said to Joan. She agreed and so we phoned her - and in about 10 minutes Carol arrived.

She's never left really.

She came to work for us while she was still at school, at weekends and during school holidays, and right from the start she was really useful – quick to learn and always willing. Without a doubt she was very bright – I think she got about eight 'O' and two 'A' levels, but when she left school she came to work for us full time for a year. The idea was that she would then go full time to Pershore College of Horticulture for suitable, high level qualifications. That was where we'd been for a few courses - but we'd got no fancy qualifications!*

Obviously however, that meant we would lose her for two or three years and she was already too useful to lose! We were chewing it all over at breakfast one day and I said to Joan

"What on earth are we going to do when Carol goes to college? - because we'll never find another Carol!"

As it turned out, Carol answered us herself. After work one day, she asked if she could have a word with us both.

"I've been talking to Mum and Dad....and we wondered how you're going to manage here once I've gone to college?"

"So do we!" we said.

"Well, how do you think it would be if I went just on a day-release course and worked here the rest of the week?"

"Well that'd be great - if you don't mind?" - and so that's what she did.

For a couple of years Carol worked for us with just one day a week at college, and we all benefited from what she was learning. After that, she worked here full time and didn't go back to college. Today, Carol looks back at that time with just a little regret, although she still cannot see that there was really any alternative:

"I'd have loved to have gone to college properly and got a real qualification, but I felt that I couldn't go full time because I would probably have lost my job at the nursery."

As I've said, that was sort of true enough – by that stage we couldn't do without the sort of help Carol was providing, so if she had gone to college full time, we would just have had to have employed a replacement – and so by the time she came back out of college there may well not have been a job here for her.

However, after about another year, Joan was nearing retirement and we were having to think about it all again. We knew that Claude Palmer, a nurseryman who had a wholesale business at St. Johns near Worcester not very far away, had got his eye on Carol, who by that time got on very well with everybody in the nursery trade and was becoming well thought of in the area. Once Joan had retired, there'd be just me running the show and so perhaps there would be a space at the top? So I said to Joan:

"I think we ought to offer Carol a partnership or she'll be getting picked up by somebody else and so we will lose her......"

---

* In fact Joan Bradshaw already had qualifications from the Midland Agricultural College at Sutton Bonnington, in 1937-8. She gained College Diplomas and Certificates in both *Dairying* and *Poultry*, but the outbreak of war prevented her from going on to gain a National Diploma.
(Her father, O.V.G.Bradshaw, had attended Harper-Adams Agricultural College in 1905-6 and gained a Diploma in *Agriculture, Book-Keeping, Dairying, Mathematics* and *Veterinary Hygiene*.)

*Carol Tozer
and her Morris Traveller,
with Sara Skinner
who lived in Bamford Close
and had a horse stabled with J&J.*

May 1979

Looking towards the main gate and the paddock filled with new stock

Some of our new stock!

New Management

In 1978 Joan retired officially and so we had already discussed our plans with Carol. Unsurprisingly, she was very keen and so, after all the details and finances were finally worked out, that's just what we did and Carol bought into the partnership.

I carried on of course, with Carol running it alongside me and with Cath Lockley still there, reliable and hardworking as always.

In 1980 Carol married her long-term boyfriend, Rollin Nicholls, dashing off on their honeymoon in Rollin's 1933 Austin Seven Box Saloon. The next year they bought a house in St.Johns, on the south side of Worcester. Rollin was working for his father's firm, so Carol was commuting to Guarlford each day.

However, the other big event for her in 1980 was that she finally bought me out. It was all completed at the end of the financial year and so on 1st April 1980 she finally owned Grange Farm Nursery herself. Carol remembers that time quite clearly:

"I felt it was all a big achievement - although, from day to day, nothing had changed really. Jo was still working part time at the Nursery, as were Cath and Tom, with Joan often around with helpful advice. It was Tom McCarry who had always done Joan & Jo's books and he carried on for a couple more years while he taught me how to look after the accounts and book-keeping properly.

The recession then came along of course and Rollin had to find himself another job, so he re-trained, gaining an HND at Pershore College of Horticulture. He worked with Homebase as a Garden Centre Manager for over ten years.

We would have liked to have both worked together at the Nursery, but it was still early days and we didn't want to put all our eggs into one basket...."

In the Spring of 1981, Carol and I decided that we'd like to have a stall at the Three Counties Show that summer, so we started planning for it. Joan and I still had our caravan at that time, so we thought it would make a good 'office' for the stand – or a shelter in case it rained!

It went quite well, and it didn't rain. So Carol was keen to do it again the next year, which we did thereafter.

As time went on, I took less part in it all of course, but I still kept an eye on things....

Jo, lurking within tent

Retirement!

After working with Carol part-time for about five years, I finally retired properly in the summer of 1985.

Joan and our friends laid on a really good party for me out in our garden and oh, so many friends turned up! It was lovely weather too and it was a fantastic day all round. I did get a little tight, though…...

Audry & Pam were at the bar.

There's Donald, John Tozer, Mary Lamb, Cath, Gordon and Margaret Earp and others too…

Below there's Dorothy Robotham, David & Pat my cousin, and Eileen my aunt.

Life At The Top

Clearly Carol had the business sense to make a good go of it and the Nursery was blossoming. Carol tells us how it was for her:

"The business paid me quite well, but we still needed Rollin's regular salary to help pay the mortgage - especially over January and February when business was very quiet."

Then in 1985 Carol decided to have a formal stand at the Three Counties Show and she really enjoyed the experience, learning a lot about how it all went on. What is more, her display attracted the attention of an official of the Royal Horticultural Society, who afterwards sent her a letter suggesting that next year she should apply for a stand at the Chelsea Flower Show. Well, we all thought that was wonderful of course, but in the end it never happened, as Carol explains:.

"No, it didn't - not because I didn't want to, but by that time we'd found that I was pregnant with our first child, Rowena. I couldn't take maternity leave, so things were looking rather difficult. Over the next few years I did try to juggle things and to keep all the balls in the air, but it really was the hardest time for me, feeling guilty about the children - Ashley had come along in 1990 - while working to keep the business going as well."

"During this period, Rollin was at Pershore College and he also became a house-husband, which was quite brave of him as it was quite unusual in those days. This allowed much more flexibility with our children and family commitments. So I was able to be properly back at the Nursery full time - and with a clear conscience once more."

Meanwhile, in 1987 Carol and her Nursery were back at the Three Counties Garden Show with the experience of 1985's show and the encouragement of the RHS's representative under her belt.

With a great deal of careful planning and preparation, the Grange Farm Nurseries' display was entered in the Spring Garden Show for the first time....
- and gained their first Bronze Award!

This also gained the Nursery (GFN) a good deal of useful local publicity and henceforth has competed at the Spring Gardening Show every year, with very satisfying results, as shown below:

	1987: Bronze			1990: Silver;
1991: Gold;	1992: Gold;	1993: Gold;	1994: Gold;	1995: Gold;
1996: SilverGilt;	1997: SilverGilt;	1998: Silver;	1999: Silver;	2000: Bronze;
2001: SilverGilt;	2002: Silver;	2003: Silver;	2004: Silver;	2005: SilverGilt;
2006: Silver;	2007: Gold;	2008: Gold;	2009: Gold;	2010: Gold*
2011: Gold;	2012: SilverGilt			

* In 2010, celebrating 25 years of the show, GFN was also awarded the *'People's Award for the Best Floral Exhibit in the Marquee'*.

Not only that, there were also three Silver Awards gained at the Three Counties' Autumn Show, so GFN was well known locally - and further away as well - and so a number of articles in the national press have followed.

In August 1994, the *Nurseryman and Garden Centre* magazine carried a full two-page article entitled 'A FAMILY SHOW WORTH SEEING'. (see Appx. 4)

In February 2005, GFN was the *Telegraph*'s 'NURSERY OF THE WEEK'.

(see Appx. 5)

In March 2008, a rather more prestigious journal, *The Lady,* looked in a personal way at Carol's career, entitled 'THE CONSTANT GARDENER' – with just the one factual error!

(see Appx. 6)

In July 2010, *Worcestershire Life* fronted its coverage of the Three Counties' Gardening Show, 'IT'S ALL ABOUT GARDENING', with a description of Carol's display in the Floral Marquee. (see Appx. 7)

In March 2012, The Independent listed GFN as number 21 out of 'THE BEST 50 GARDEN CENTRES'. (see Appx. 8)

THE ROYAL HORTICULTURAL SOCIETY

Established 1804 Incorporated 1809

GOLD MEDAL

AWARDED TO   GRANGE FARM NURSERIES LTD

1991 MALVERN SPRING GARDENING SHOW

For an exhibit of   HARDY TREES, SHRUBS & OTHER PLANTS

The Nursery held an Open Day in 1988 in aid of St. John Ambulance
- and Cath poses for the camera.

114

In 2007, Rollin's mother died and shortly afterwards he decided that the time was right to join Carol and work full time at the Nursery. Carol was pleased about this of course.

"Yes, because by this time the Nursery had really settled down to being a large, stable business, giving us a reliable income - even through the winter! - and so we were happy to both be committed to it full time. We'd have loved to have done it earlier, and could have done, but we didn't know how things would turn out.

So we were, and still are, both enjoying it all together, with our team alongside us. The 'Support Team' that had got together when the children were very young and times were hard - our parents and friends - are still mostly around and that's why it all works as well as it does.

Cath was already working at the Nursery, then soon afterwards we gained another real support when Shane joined us, fresh from school. Oh - he's officially called Mark Baddeley, but we all call him Shane. In fact, only just recently Cath was asked if Mark was around and she said no, nobody of that name works here!"

"And then there's Rollin's sister, Lois Speedy, who has a real gift on the artistic arrangement side of things.

It's Lois that has the greatest input for the shows' displays - and the list of awards over the years is a testament to this.

The other good piece of evidence of how smoothly things work can be seen when Rollin and I have to be off site – and everything just carries on just like clockwork.

A great team!"

Grange Farm Nursery's Display at the 2010 Three Countries Show, where it won a Gold Award and the People's Award for the Best Floral Exhibit in the Marquee.

115

I must say that I'm pleased with the way things have gone in Carol and Rollin's hands. Joan was pleased too, and today the standards are higher than ever.

Grange Farm Nursery's Display at the 2011 Three Countries Show where it yet again won a Gold Award

"My greatest satisfaction" says Carol, "has been the fact that I am a profitable business woman, able to support myself independently and provide income and jobs for other people. Selling plants is an industry that I love."

The Team: *Rollin, Lois, Carol, Shane, Cath - and Jo.*   *30th August 2012*

Photo by Jim Speedy

Passing it on…..

Carol sums up what her involvement in the Nursery has meant to her.

"One of the most important things I learned from Jo and Joan when I left school to work for them, was what it means to really earn your living, what's called a 'work ethic'. I soon saw how important it is to be able to be relied upon, to turn up for work on time, not to take advantage of your employers' good will and to be willing to do that extra bit every now and again. This has all stood me in good stead throughout my working life, and it was the two Joans who set me the good example in the first place.

I soon wanted to pass this on if I could and so now, each year we have a pupil from The Chase or Hanley High School for a week's work experience. This must be a bit better organised than it was in Jo's day because it all works well and I feel it's worth while.

We've also employed lots of local young people from the area over the years, including Ellie Ward from Guarlford, who has since gone on to train as a lawyer; and Rosie Goldman, who is training for a degree at Pershore; Olivia Harrison, who has gone on to be an architect, and currently John Adeney works here, who is intending to become an officer in the Army
.

Mostly they work here at weekends and during school holidays of course, and we've seen lots of youngsters passing through, naturally including our own children, Rowena and Ashley. The Nursery provides them with useful earnings as pupils and students, as well as being a good taste of the employment ladder. For some it seems to help with their self-confidence too - it's REAL work experience.

Now, whether either Rowena or Ashley will eventually want us to pass it on to them, we don't know, but I do think that Grange Farm Nursery has been a very valuable and enjoyable experience for just everyone who has been involved in it."

Carol Nicholls
June 2012

117

Chapter 10
PUBS & MOTORS

Pubs I Have Enjoyed

Over the years, I've been in quite a few pubs really. Maybe the very first one I remember was *The Chequers* in Pershore, where my grandparents were landlord and lady. They were Charles and Harriet Newell and I can remember visiting them there when I was about five years old - but the pub has gone now. They completely flattened it – a real shame because it was lovely, really old pub and once it's been demolished you can't bring it back.

Then there was *The Star* in Upton upon Severn, where my father's sister, Lillian and her husband Jim Gee was the landlord. That's still there of course, and from about seven years of age I used to help Uncle Jim and Auntie Lil in the pub. Well, what I mean is I visited them and I'd get on with their children, Maggie and Albert, of course. But by the time I was about ten I could pull a mean pint, I can tell you. They wouldn't let you do that today, would they?

They had floods in Upton of course, but I don't remember it getting into the pub early on. Ah – but I do remember sitting on the steps of the pub and feeding the swans as they paddled up the street in the floods. And then in 1947 it did come in and they were very badly flooded, although it was Mr.& Mrs Barden who were the landlords by that time.

A big adventure for us children happened on the river. The Severn is close by of course and Maggie and I used to go rowing along the river. All on our own, two young girls with no life-jackets or rescue launches, just Maggie and me. Anyway, there we were rowing along and I lost an oar, so we were into the bushes that were hanging over from the banks, looking for the oar, when we found a body. Well, we hurried back and told Jumpin' Harry, the local boatman. He was the man to tell, because he knew what to do and he'd get 7/6d for each body he retrieved from the river. He rowed off but soon came back and said he couldn't find it. Now, Maggie wouldn't go with him because she had more sense, so I went and we found it. Harry tied a rope around its chest, hung on, and told me to row back to Upton.

"Don't you go so jumpin' fast my girl – it'll fall to jumpin' bits!" Anyway, we got back and he heaved the body onto his handcart and took it up to Upton's mortuary. I found it all very interesting, but I was told that I was lucky that the eels didn't come out and get me…..

It turned out that the man had jumped off the bridge at Stourport to kill himself.

After that there were the pubs I came across in the Army and I've mentioned some of those already, including the one along the railway near Dering Lines Army Camp. This was near the town of Brecon, but I don't recall its name now.

Then there was the **Cound Inn** to which we could walk from Cound Hall. A friendly pub it was for us young girls who were a fair way away from home.

Also there was **The Boathouse** in New Street, Shrewsbury. The attraction for us there, during the war, were the fry-ups they would do for us, as I've said before.

After the war we would sometimes drop into *The Blue Bell* at Callow End because it was local to us, but it is **The Three Kings** at Church End in Hanley Castle that seems to have stood the test of time for me.

I remember the innkeepers, Fred & Ethel Roberts when I was a kid and their son George used to tease me when I went in there with my dad. George really was a jovial character with a good sense of humour. In fact it was George, much later on, that gave me the martingale that's hanging on the wall behind me now.

They used to hold the Gamekeepers' Supper there every year, and also a Badger Supper (they were eaten many years ago), but ladies weren't invited that evening – although perhaps it was just that no women ever wanted to go....?

Ethel Roberts outside her pub in the 1940s.

Sue Roberts has since found the old sign pole and brackets and it has more decorative ironwork than appear in this (restored) picture.

More recently, Russell Taylor and his wife Pat, who were good friends, and I used to go there and for a time we used to like to sample George's draught sherry. It was cheap, but really was potent stuff and it's a wonder it didn't kill us! It did make us both pretty badly ill once, so never again – we went back onto the beer. They still did the smoked badger ham sandwiches at that time - and even roast hedgehog, but I never tried the hedgehog.

Whenever Russell and I went in – and that was before Nell's Cottage was added to the pub, when there was only the two little front rooms: the Smoke & Darts Room to the left and the Snug to the right with the sliding door – there was always old Tom Harris, a local farm worker, supping his cider next to the bar. We three got on very well, with lots of banter and laughing throughout the evening. Russell and I were recalling old Tom only the other day.

Then, about 20 years ago or so, I'm afraid that good old George died, leaving Sheila with their son and daughter Sue and Dave, and she bravely carried on. I remember that Sheila used to play a mean game of tennis, but she also ran the pub well and kept order despite all of us! She was a cheery soul too and she kept going for a very long time indeed, still pulling pints until quite recently – although still charging for them in pounds, shillings and pence, while Sue really took care of the money.

Some years ago, for possibly the first time since the pub moved a few yards along the road a few hundred years ago, a change was made! Nell Creese, the very old lady who lived next door, died and the Roberts were able to expand sideways. Thankfully, Sue has integrated Nell's Bar perfectly and it all still feels right, just as it always has.

Sue and Jo, with Lucy the spaniel, outside The Three Kings, on 3rd May, 2012

Photo by John

Last year, 2011, provided an opportunity for lots of extra jollity at the pub, and fund-raising for local charities, as it was the 100th anniversary of the Roberts' reign at The Three Kings

- and I've been going in there for 80 of them!

The Swan at Newland used to be a favourite, especially when the hounds met there. I do still go there on occasion, maybe for lunch with friends, and it's still got good food and drink. What's more, it's not been mucked about like so many old pubs have been.

The other Swan has always had good food too, in my memory anyway. **The Swan** at Hanley on the old drovers' road must have been there for many hundreds of years. When I first went there, the chap who ran it had previously worked for The Duke, that's David Nicholson, who was a well known trainer of chasers at Condicote, so we had things in common right from the start. His wife had a horse she called '*Ooey*' or something, which Joan and I used to look after. We had many happy times in that pub and looking back it seems as if there was a party in the bar every night! There's pictures of The Swan in Chapter 8 because the Hunt often met there.

However, the brewery who owned it thought they knew better and closed it for a while in order to tart it all up. Our friends had to go at the same time and, despite a local shop keeper's hopes to go there – and I think that she would have been very good – the brewery brought in a new landlord and it's all very different now. I don't go there much any more as it's a bit too expensive for me – although they do some rather good take-away fish 'n chips!

One of my all-time favourites is **The Duke of York,** despite it being some nine miles away, which is a bit far to be our 'local'. Sometime in the 1980s, Joan and I went with Mollie Horton, that's John Horton's mother, to a demonstration of Sam Barr's horses at Hartpury. It was in a big barn, in the middle of winter - and we were frozen stiff. Driving back in the Land-Rover didn't warm up much either and so as we came round the corner we saw the Duke and we turned in on the off-chance of it being able to warm us up. Well, as we came in, there was the biggest open fire you ever did see and we were welcomed by Pam the landlady, and soon settled down in front of the fire and started to thaw out. David, her husband got us some lovely soup and hot rolls and it all turned out really well.

So, we've been back there ever since. We used to have our Christmas party there, with 12 or 15 of our friends. But then Pam and David left and moved to Leominster.

We were devastated, but then Sheila and Dave took over and so it was different of course, but just as good. Sheila was just born to be a landlady and we had happy times there once more.

One year they organised a 'Country Fair' in aid of charity and we took part in the fun and games with the dogs.

Jo with Honey, who did NOT want to 'Walk the Plank'.

Jo with Nell, who got 1st Prize in the 'Veterans' class

Sadly however, after only a few years Dave died. Sheila carried on for two or three more years, but it was too much for her on her own so she gave up. The cook carried on with the new young couple who took over, but it all turned out badly. It's an interesting tale, but not one I should tell here, I think.

Anyway, The Duke is all back on form again with Miles at the helm, I'm very glad to say, and it's a happy pub once more.

The Bluebell at the end of the Guarlford straight was a cosy pub, but for me it was spoiled recently by some big firm that changed it completely.

However, also on the Guarlford Road, midway along, is **The Green Dragon** and, although it's been expanded, it's still a real pub with friendly staff – and Sue's been there for 25 years now! I do enjoy a light lunch there with good, home-cooked food.

I've talked before about **The Plough and Harrow** of course, which is I suppose our nearest pub, and here's a picture of Joan in the landau on her birthday outside the Plough, where Gill swapped places with Rosie. It's still a nice pub, but it's changed from when we used to go there frequently and it's now mainly a restaurant - expensive, but very good.

It's closed at the moment, for some reason - but we'll see what happens. It's too good to lose.

Sometimes I still visit **The Chase** just above Colwall – I go there for some lunch with Log every now and again and they are very friendly there, with good food too. All those steps are bit much for me nowadays, but it's worth it.

It must have been back in the 1950s when I first went into the **Plume of Feathers** on Castlemorton Common. I had been down to Longdon Marshes cutting watercress with Harry and Humphrey Bladder and we went in, but it was very dark in there, just a few candles lit. Many places still had no electricity at that time. We could see some local men sitting around the fire, looking round at us, and then the landlord lifted a candlestick up to see us a bit better and

asked *"Oo be you then? Whaddya want?"* We left.

We've been in again more recently of course, usually for a bite of lunch after having walked the dogs on the common.

Jo & Joan, with Joan's niece-in-law Gill, her children Toby & Lindsay, together with Jo's spaniel Nell after a walk on the Common in May 1993

Photo by John

But then there was another period when we didn't go in for a time and I'll always remember why. We'd walked into the bar and were ordering a couple of scotches, but it was rather difficult to make myself heard over the volume of the tele in the bar. I think we were the only customers in there and so I asked the landlord to turn it off, or at least down a good bit.

"No. I'm watching it" he said. That surprised me and annoyed me too, so I said that we would leave.

"That's your prerogative to do so" he said, and I told him that it was also my prerogative to never come in again while he was the landlord – but I didn't have to wait long as he'd gone within six months, and I wasn't surprised.

It's recently been closed, I don't know why, but it's open again now I'm glad to say as it's a lovely country pub and usefully located near to the common.

Also close to Castlemorton Common is the ***Farmers Arms***, another good country pub which we've enjoyed.

I like to drop into the ***White Lion*** in Upton because when Joan and I were doing some shopping there on a Saturday morning we would enjoy taking a break there and it's still very convenient to get a good cup of nice coffee in their very comfortable front lounge.

Where else? Well there was ***The Crown*** and ***The White Horse*** at Exford, from where Joan and I could hear the local hunt's hounds singing early in the morning – and that reminds me of ***The Hark to Bounty*** at Slaidburn in the Forest of Bowland. I think that Bounty must have been a lead hound in the local hunt of course. A lovely pub, with lots of character.

Margaret & Gorden Earp at the Gardener's Arms in Alerton

We've been into so many pubs over the years:
    good, bad, and indifferent;
        clean, dirty and just about acceptable;
            friendly, unfriendly and uninterested…

But there's nothing like a good, traditional English pub.
            And long may they last!

Military Motors

There's been lots of vehicles in my life of course, but they don't stay in my memory like horses do. There's no character, no relationship with a lump of metal. But I've done a fair few tens of thousands of miles behind the wheel, as I've told you already.

So I really don't remember what it was that I was taught to drive in. Neither can I recall much about the bread-vans I drove.

Later, in the Army, I can tell you for certain that I drove lots of great big Bedford trucks, and Guys and Morris trucks too, most of them were open when we drove them, with the windscreens tucked safely away behind to protect them in transit – but not us. Later there were articulated lorries, and that's when I really learned how to reverse with a trailer, a skill that's been useful ever since.

There were also all sorts of military vehicles too and I've already mentioned the one I hated, the Quad. That was awful, especially in winter!

But there were also Bren-gun carriers, armoured cars, tanks and even ducks – but we never drove them through water!

General Motors DUKW – the American amphibious truck: the 'Duck'

We didn't like the American vehicles that much. Nothing to do with them being left-hand drive, that was no problem for us at all, and even the throttle pedal between the clutch and brake pedal was alright. No, it was just the way they handled – or didn't handle...... although the Chevvys and the Studebaker troop-carrier were OK, in fact they were rather luxurious we thought at the time. Maybe we would see them differently now?

And then there were the Jeeps. Now they really were crude, uncomfortable things. Swing round the corner too fast and you fell out because there were no doors and not much to hang onto either. In fact we nearly did lose one of our drivers when she fell out around a corner in a Jeep. She was alright, but it was a nasty experience for her and the Jeep ended up in the ditch on the other side of the road.

Our Land-Rovers after the war were much better.

Willys-Overland Jeep. Over 30% of Jeeps built during the war were supplied to British and Soviet forces

Land-Rovers

An old friend ours was John Robotham, who used to live at the Cherry Orchard, a nearby farm in Guarlford where Liz and Dr. Peter Mayner now live. After the war, John had his own place, Newhouse Farm, in Hollybush, near Eastnor, but was still interested in motoring. In fact, he had just finished building what he considered to be the best of all British sports cars - a Frazer Nash. Not just assembling, or restoring one - building one from scratch! He was well pleased with his latest creation, calling over to show it to us. I remember that - it was the real McCoy, with cycle wings, bonnet strap - the full works - and it went like stink too! John was like a puppy with two tails with it.

On another occasion, Colin went over to John's at Eastnor to see quite a different vehicle. The Robothans had just bought a new workhorse for the farm: a Land Rover. I was also interested of course, but for some reason couldn't go with Colin that time – but, unlike Colin, I was later to own a number of Land-Rovers throughout my farming years and beyond.

John took Colin out for a run in it and finally swung back into the farmyard. Now, usually the passenger seat was occupied by his sister Dorothy, who would open the door to receive their very enthusiastic puppy onto her lap. However, when Colin opened the door it was to rather unexpectedly see a gigantic salivating boxer dog heading straight at him at a few hundred mph.... Possibly unsurprisingly, he promptly slammed the door shut again, whereupon the poor dog cannoned into the side of the Land Rover, seriously rocking the vehicle and re-profiling the passenger door forever. The dog bounced back off - and then just wandered away shaking its head....

However, Colin needed a stiff whisky before he could set to apologising properly to Dorothy and enquiring about the damage to both machine and beast, but it seems there was no real harm done and it was all just put down to experience – and a good tale to tell Joan and me when he got back to Guarlford.

John Robotham never married, living with his sister Dorothy and their mother until he very sadly died prematurely in about 1970 from what was called *'Farmer's Lung'** in those days.

Not long after that we had Land-Rovers ourselves, all short wheelbases. We had a couple of Series IIs and then a Series III with carpets! Bloody silly that was too – they kept all the water in and it rusted like billy-o. And then we had a couple of Range-Rovers, which were a lot more comfortable, although we did still keep a really old Land-Rover for quite a time afterwards, but not for use on the road.

Mind you, I'd made a good deal with Joan's nephew, John, once he'd got his driving license. If he did the maintenance on the Land-Rover, he could use it when he needed to. He did a fair bit on the Series III, including replacing the clutch at one time, but he didn't get to use it much as it was our main working vehicle and usually we couldn't do without it.

*Farmer's Lung A hypersensitivity pneumonitis induced by the inhalation of biologic dusts coming from hay dust or mould spores or other agricultural products.

Jo's and a friend's Range-Rovers outside Grange Farm.

But I do remember that he borrowed our Land-Rover one weekend to take his girlfriend Gill up into the hills to propose to her - which clearly worked. Oh, and then many years later he borrowed it and the Rice horsebox to recover his bike, but John remembers that occasion better than I do:

"I was riding my Ariel Square-Four back from my Club's AGM and was going down into Bewdley when a car way up ahead suddenly swerved into a turning on the right, causing a series of emergency stops behind. I stopped OK, but with my front tyre out on the centre line, when a Morris Traveller came the other way, with its driver looking over his shoulder at what was going on……. He clipped my front wheel, swerved left, through a stone wall and down into a ditch. He'd wrecked my front forks, and just about wrote off the Morris – which was out on its very first trip after having been totally rebuilt.

I pushed the bike into the hedge and hitched a lift to Guarlford to borrow Jo's Landie and trailer. I then drove it to Hartlebury to pick up Gill and we went back to collect the bike. Returning through Stourport-on-Severn, the front nearside wheel came off and bounced off ahead of us, as the wheel-hub hit the road. The large L-R wheel bounced off the curb, rolled over the verge and heavily hit a cherry-blossom tree – completely covering a little old lady, who had been sitting underneath it, in pretty pink cherry-blossom.

While Gill calmed her down and dusted her off, I set about trying to get the Landie's wheel back on, which was so deeply sunk into the tarmac that the jack wouldn't fit underneath. I did it in the end though and we got back with just 3 nuts on each wheel.

Jo thought it might have been the result of someone having been interrupted half way through trying to steal the wheels?

I've had one or two Land-Rovers of my own since then."

127

Tractors

As I've told you already, I drove a Fordson tractor for Gaffer Tolley, but it was the Fergie Grey that I remember best of all. We had one of our own later on and it was a useful, reliable machine and I got on with it very well indeed, for many years.

Ferguson TE20

Jo on her Fergie Grey at Guarlford in the late 1980s

We used our Fergie for just about everything - for mowing, ploughing and harrowing, and also for turning and wallying the hay. It towed trailers and our dray, as well as having a transport box on the back, in which we could shift bales or salt-licks down the fields. A big, long flat belt from the PTO (power take-off - a pulley at the back) drove our circular saw and also rolled oats for the horses.

We still had our old Fergie through to the 1980s, but I can't remember just where it went to in the end.

Jo and Harry in deep mud

In 1989 I had some work to do down in the fields and so I borrowed a David Brown tractor - and that was pure luxury! It was over a hot few days, but it had a roof, so I was in the shade. It was a lot more modern than my old Fergie of course, with power steering and brakes too.

Jo in the bottom field
on the borrowed DB 995

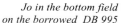

And then I really moved up in the world - with Power Mowing!

Jo on her new Westwood
S600 Garden Tractor

129

Cars

After the war, my father had a Morris Eight and I used to drive it too. However, the winter of 1946-47 was really very bad indeed and I can remember us getting stuck in a snowdrift across the road and having to dig ourselves out, with the aid of a young chap who came out to help.

Jo and an unknown helper digging her father's Morris 8 out of the snow in January 1947

I've already told you about our first car, the 1928 Riley 9 Lynx that we called 'Barkis'. That did us well both on the farm and on the road and it was quite some time before we replaced it. We then had a saloon Riley, a Kestrel, which happened to be available when Barkis' big end went. However, we didn't keep that one for very long and we soon part-exchanged it for a Ford van, which was really far more useful.

Joan in Barkis, outside the Stonehouse in 1947.
A plate from Joan's horse, Robin, can be seen on the radiator.

Then we swapped the van for a Series II Land-Rover. At about that time we also had a drop-head Morris Minor, as by that stage we were moving towards having both a 'work' vehicle as well as a rather more civilised 'leisure' vehicle. We were out shopping with the Morris in Worcester and our Alsatian, Judy, was stretched out on the back seat. A young man was passing by and, admiring the dog, rested his hand on the car – whereupon he very nearly got his nose bitten off, as Judy saw it as being her job to protect our property! Fortunately, we were just coming back and managed to calm things down.

So of course, as I've mentioned before, we had Series IIs and a Series III Land-Rover for work on and around the farm, but afterwards we had a couple of Range-Rovers which were a lot more comfortable, but no cheaper to run. Just for use around the farm we hung onto an old Land-Rover and then we got a very rusty Mini Pickup – but these would never have passed the newly introduced MoT !

After all this time I cannot remember in what order the cars came, but we did have two or three Fords, including a Ford estate of some sort, and then a nearly new Ford Consul in an off-white colour with red seats. It didn't suit us very well as it made the passengers feel sick, rolling and wallowing as it did. So we sold it to Joan's brother, Colin, who ran it for a while. It blew up while he had it and so he put a reconditioned engine in and sold it shortly afterwards. He never liked it, but his wife, Peggy, did as it was so much more warm and comfortable than Colin's 'vintage' cars.

I used to have our Land-Rovers serviced by a really good chap in Great Whitley and he knew we were looking out for another saloon car. He had a silver Lancia Flavia saloon in stock, recommended it, and so we bought it as it was a good bargain at the time. It was a good car, if rather 'up-market' for me and every time I got into I felt I should be very smart and properly dressed. I enjoyed driving it, getting about 110mph out it of once, and then when I went to my old school re-union they all thought I'd come into some money or something. So then I sold another car to Colin and he really appreciated the Lancia's engineering and its performance. And then his brother-in-law, Cecil, bought one too. Eventually Cecil sold his to Colin's younger son, Ian, so for a time Lancias were very much in the family!

Sadly, Colin hit black ice in our old Lancia on Cannock Chase one Boxing Day and, although it seemed to be only slightly damaged, it had to be written off.

My pals, and Colin too of course, used to take the opportunity to try each others' vehicles when the opportunities arose. So that's how I got to drive a Morgan. Now, despite living for most of my life within a few miles of the Morgan factory, I'd never tried one before, so when Colin's lad, John, turned up in an ivory coloured Plus 4 well, I just had to have a go. Oh it was alright I suppose, but not much good for doing anything useful really...

Jo in John's Morgan +4   August 1975

After that there was a run of Volkswagens for us – the Passat model seemed to suit us best and we had a very good hatchback for a time. Sadly they stopped making that version, so we had two Passat Estates after that. Joan also had a VW Golf Estate for a short while, but she didn't like it at all.

I used to buy our cars from Charlie Richards of Hereford Motors. I'd known Charlie from when he was just a junior salesman and he worked himself up to the top. Our first VW Passat from him was fine, we liked it and so we later replaced it with an estate, but then the horn kept going off at any time of day or night – it was the built-in burglar alarm system that was to blame. People kept coming into the pub to tell me that it had gone off again in the car-park – and that really annoyed me, although because it seemed to always go off outside the Duke of York, they seemed to think it was much funnier than I did. Once it even went off while I was driving down the Guarlford straight, with the horn going and all the lights flashing! So I took it back to Charlie who said he'd fix it – but despite all his efforts it kept on doing it. I asked him to just disconnect it altogether, but then the central locking system wouldn't work if he did that! Anyway, one night it went off twice and there I was going down in my dressing down at three o'clock in the morning to turn it off and so I phoned up Charlie first thing the next morning to tell him that it really was the final straw...... So he phoned me back to say that he'd got a choice of two Passats for me - one was black and the other one was silver. Well, I didn't want to go round driving a hearse, so I went for the silver one. That was another estate and two litres, whereas the old one was a 1.8 litre and had done a higher mileage, so we chopped it in with an extra £200 and got ourselves a good one. Charlie sent it off to the auction – caveat emptor – but he looked after us alright.

At that time I had all my cars serviced by Robin Milne at Hanley Castle, in the very barn where Dave Roberts has his workshop now. Robin really was very good at his job, and very good to us, too. He always fixed it and never charged us more than he needed to, so we never took our cars anywhere else, right up until he retired. He's gone now, I'm sorry to say.
(Poor old Robin did tend to suffer from people who got him mixed up with A.A. Milne - and called him Christopher.)

Currently I'm running a CR-V Honda, which suits me down to the ground. Not very exciting, but it does what I want at my age.

Bikes

Bicycles have never really appealed to me, although I've ridden them of course. I had one when I was first in the Army and rode it from our billets to work, although I hadn't got any lights on it. So I was riding it back one night and a copper stepped out in front of me. I'd have been in trouble, so I swerved around him and pedalled off as fast as I could. I got away with that, but then a bit later I left it outside the pub and it was stolen. My fault of course, but I couldn't afford another bicycle. Anyway, we were soon moved to Cound Hall and I didn't need one after that.

In 1999 we had a sponsored bicycle ride for the local churches. It was raising money for the 'Worcester, Dudley & District Historic Churches Trust' and I rode a bicycle which I had borrowed from Gill Ferris.

There were more of these rides, although I didn't ride in them, but there's more about this in the next chapter.

Jo on Gill's mountain bike

Motorcycles were more fun, although Joan was put off them from the moment she first met me on my BSA and I've never owned a motorcycle since.

However, I do remember Joan's nephew, John, offering me a ride on his Ariel motorcycle in the 1980s - and I called his bluff! I had a very nice little ride around the lanes on it, but I think John was very relieved when I brought it back in one piece.

More recently, he arrived on a new bike - a giant BMW. I don't remember him offering me a go on this one though.....

Jo sitting on John's BMW R1150
- but just sitting ... .. Photo by John

HGVs

For my 80th birthday, Gill Ferris treated me to a day driving heavy goods vehicles, including an articulated lorry. We made quite a day of it, with Joan, John & Barbara Horton, Don & Barbara Hill and Rosie McCarry, but ironically Gill couldn't make it herself as she was at work.

It was all at Throckmorton airfield and we met the chap there with the artic. He showed me where all the modern controls were and then he said *"OK – let's go for a ride"* – so we did.

It was quite easy with the power steering, power brakes – and with really comfortable seats! What's more I could see everything very well, sitting so high up, with a wide, high windscreen and those giant mirrors. It was dead easy and good fun. We drove up and down the airfield, reversed around a bit and I reversed it into a garage. Successfully, of course.

Jo at the wheel of an articulated truck on Throckmorton Airfield

Ladies Driving Challenge

Another interesting day behind the wheel was again at Throckmorton airfield, but this was a charity fund raising event in support of Marie Curie Nurses. There were dozens of women there, and we were driving artics, buses, trucks, fire-engines, tractors and cars. Usually they had a tank there, but this time they couldn't make it, not that I was sorry as they were a real devil to get in and out of – I remember that from my time driving them in the war.

Driving the car was the least unusual, but the tests in it were really challenging, reversing through tight cones and other tests. It was great fun, and everyone should have a go. Gill was with me that time, but she wouldn't have a go herself and was helping with the marshalling instead.

Chapter 11
RETIREMENT

Caravans

When I eventually retired in 1985, we had far more time together at home and for me to help get the garden into shape, which I've always enjoyed doing.

However, we decided that we'd have some holidays too, so we bought a caravan, because it was easier with the dogs. Joan had got her little long haired daschunds at the time, Tansy & Katy.

We went across to Suffolk, we went into Wales and we went down to Exmoor quite a lot, which we particularly loved. We used to walk miles and miles and miles. It was usually into a pub in the evening for a meal - The Royal Oak in Winsford was particularly good - or maybe it was in one of the other villages, I can't really remember the name of it now.

We had some lovely holidays down there - we found the people very friendly and we got on with them very well.

One time we'd taken the caravan in a hurry – we'd suddenly found we could go. So we quickly packed everything into it and went off down to Suffolk. We stopped in a vineyard at Clare, which was lovely, just perfect.

We parked there, unhooked, and I went off to get the water. We'd got a roller-barrel with a handle - only I hadn't got the handle. With a handle they're dead easy to move, but without the handle they're damned difficult. I was struggling with this barrel and the man standing in the caravan opposite said *"Would you like to borrow my handle?"*

So I borrowed his handle and got the water and took the handle back. We could now make some tea, but then Joan said *"Oh Lord - we've come without the kettle! Oh well, I'll just have to boil the water in a saucepan."* So she went to light the gas - and we hadn't got any matches.

So I had to go crawling over to this chap, apologise profusely and beg.

"Could I have a match please?"

"Yes, of course my dear, you can have some matches" he said with a smile. He gave me half a box and said, *"You can keep those."* So back I go and we put the saucepan on and boiled the water and made two cups of tea.

We were just lying down there on our respective beds, which were one either side, and looking up Joan suddenly cried out *"Oh my God! The roof's gone!"* I looked up and the skylight was missing - we'd got a great big gaping hole. The weather was a bit.....well it was all right, I don't think there was any rain about, but we weren't very happy. But there was nothing we could do about it, this was about 9 o'clock at night, so we just settled down and camped out for the night.

"We'll have to try and find a caravan place and see if we can buy a lid." I said after we'd packed up the next morning. I measured it, but then had my doubts: '*I wonder if I'll be able to fix it on.....?*' So off we went anyway, and this is where our luck changed. About a mile out of Clare we went past a little two-pump garage, which were around in those days, and I happened to look across and at the back where there were a lot of caravans. So I stopped, backed up, and went in and asked.

"Do you have any caravan spares......please?"

"Oh yes, we do – what do you want?" and so I told them and then they said *"How would it be if you went and fetched your caravan down here and we'll do it and then you can have it back tonight, and meanwhile you two can go off an enjoy yourselves?"*

So that's what we did and we came back at night and it was done and that was that. We had a jolly good holiday after that and we had lovely weather too.

That wasn't quite the end of it all, though. Later that year we took the caravan again to Wyley Horse Trials and once more Rosemary came with us, Rosie McCarry, that is. We got down there and we were having a cup of tea when somebody noticed the skylight had gone again. It was a silly thing - it was a big square thin thing - and there was this great big gaping hole. This time the weather was definitely dodgy, it was showery, so we really had to do something about it immediately. Well we always took a spare wheel for the caravan in a plastic bag. So we took the spare wheel out of the plastic bag and chucked the wheel under the caravan and decided that we'd put this plastic bag over the hole. But how to hold it down? It was stony country around there of course, so we went on the hunt and here and there we found two or three big stones, brought them back. In those days we had a Range Rover and by letting down the tailgate I could just reach to put this plastic bag on, pinned down with the stones.

A bit later on we met two ladies on the campsite who were in the next caravan and who were looking at us rather strangely.....

"Can you please explain something for us - why you were putting stones on your caravan roof?" We told them why and they said *"We did wonder, it seemed such a strange thing to be doing."*

"Well it might be a strange thing to do - but at least it's doing the trick!" We had a laugh about it and then they made tea for us all.

Anyway when we got back I took it down to the caravan place, at Stratford Bridge on the A38, and they repaired it properly and that was that.

It was about that time that Carol and I were doing the stand at the Three Counties Show each year and the caravan came in very useful as a base for us there for a bit – in fact to start with we used the caravan on the stand itself, so it was used as a sort of office – which wasn't at all what we'd bought it for in the first place of course!

Then we had a holiday in Wales with Joan's brother Colin, his wife Peggy and their son John, and his wife Gill. Colin & Peggy had their own caravan and we had ours and John & Gill were camping with their kids Toby & Lindsay.

It was the last day of a nice holiday and we'd all been out for the day. We were coming back for a meal that Peggy and Gill would be cooking for us all. But then we decided that instead we would stop in the hotel in Dolgellau and have something to eat there.

Which we did, but on the way back I started with a tickle in my throat and by the time we got back to the caravan I'd got a full blown dose of something, almost feeling like flu. I ached all over and I was coughing and sneezing and I could hardly breathe. So I went to bed with a bottle and Joan kept me supplied with hot whisky and hot drinks, but I don't think we had a wink of sleep. It absolutely chucked it down all night with rain and it was banging on the caravan roof. Those of you who've been in caravan in a heavy storm will know exactly what I mean. It was an awful night in every way.

"*We're going home!*" I said to Joan the next morning. I still felt awful, but I still had to drive all the way home because Joan wouldn't drive with the caravan on the back. Anyway we got home safely, eventually, and I just struggled out of the car, into the house and went to bed. I was there for about three days – and so was the car and caravan, still all hitched up and dumped outside the house.

"*I never want to see that caravan ever again*" I said to Joan later on.

"*Neither do I*" she replied, feelingly. So we sold it and that was the end of our caravanning.

B&Bs - and Stalking...

After that, we decided that Bed & Breakfast was a much more civilised thing to do. That was when we joined the 'Farmhouse Holiday Guide' and we stayed with them from then on, enjoying some lovely farmhouses. We used to go for just B&B and have an evening meal somewhere out, which we found was much more relaxing because you didn't have to rush to get back in time for meal. We had some super holidays doing it that way.

We went to Scotland one year with some friends, June & Margaret, and we stayed with Arthur & Cath, a stalker and his wife on the banks of Loch Awe. We had a fabulous holiday there. Cath was a superb cook and we had super evening meals and breakfasts to die for. Arthur liked his malt whiskeys too – and I dread to think just how many bottles we got through....
(Joan used to leave her dachsies up in the bedroom while we had breakfast and Arthur used to get a sausage and take it up to the dogs, so every morning they had a sausage in bed!)

They were just lovely people and one day Arthur asked if we'd like to go with him up into the hills - and so we all said *Yes!* He said, "*Well, it means getting up at 5 o'clock.....?*" - but we'd had a lifetime of that, so we could do it again.

So Cath made us some sandwiches for later and we had a piece of toast and a cup of tea or coffee for early breakfast and off we went.

We went for miles...... Then Arthur found a stag and he said, "*There's one I must shoot, it's an old one.*" I wasn't very happy about this, but he took aim and shot it - and it dropped stone dead. It didn't know a thing. I didn't feel so bad about it after that, especially when later he showed us the damage that the stags can do with their antlers. They also have to cull them because there's too many of them and there isn't enough food for them in the winter. And then they make good food for us too of course.

We went on and he took us all over the hills and it was fantastic scenery, absolutely beautiful, but very rough going.... We'd left the little dogs in the car because Arthur said *"Those dogs will never cope with this,"* and they wouldn't have done - it was really rough.

There were deep drains and then we heard a shout and there was Margaret, one of our friends, up to her armpits in one of these ditches. She was not very big and she was nearly out of sight! So we dashed back and hoiked her out of there.

We went what seemed to me like even further on, and then he took us down to a Loch – which turned out to be not too far from where we'd parked the cars. It was idyllic: it was turning out to be beautiful day, warm and bright, and there were even deer down by the Loch side grazing and drinking. Arthur left us there to do some fly-fishing, which June, Margaret and I did, while Joan relaxed on the bank.

We'd come back to eat our sandwiches with Joan, but it was by mid-morning by then and we were all beginning to feel hungry again, so we traipsed our way back to the car, which we'd been shown by Arthur before he'd left because we'd never have found it otherwise. It had been a wonderful day already, and then lunch followed by a light nap made it all just perfect.

Then we went to the Cotswold Wild Life Park in the summer of 2000, but we weren't stalking the game there......

Photo by Jo

Friends

Retirement gave us the opportunity to spend time with friends. Di and Dorothy were very good friends who we got to know through the Nursery. We had a great deal in common with them such as the love of dogs, birds and the countryside. We had lots of days out together, at least one a week. We went walking and either had a pub lunch or a picnic depending on the time of year. We also had holidays together in places such as Dolgellau where we enjoyed walking and eating and drinking. Many a happy day was spent at their home where they had the most beautiful wild flower meadow. When I was unfortunate enough to break my wrist they came over every week to take us out for a pub meal, because by then Joan had stopped driving.

Friends closer at hand were Margaret and Gordon Earp who lived in the village who, when we first got to know them, invited us to lunch. However, that very morning, Gordon 'phoned us.

"Sorry Jo, but could you come a bit later, please? So sorry to mess you about, but it's a bit difficult – Margaret's had a little bit of a crisis in the kitchen. We do hope you don't mind too much?" He did sound embarrassed!

"No, no! Of course not, no trouble at all. About half-one then? Fine, looking forward to seeing you. Bye." In fact, we had in fact totally forgotten our luncheon appointment and as soon as I'd put the phone down, I shot into the kitchen at full speed.

"Take it off! Take all the lunch off the stove – we're going to lunch with the Earps!" and I told her what had happened.

Of course, when we knew Margaret and Gordon better we told them about this and we all had a good laugh about it. We had many happy times with them.

Of course, we always took the opportunity to go to interesting shows, and Badminton Horse Trials was always a good do, until it got just too big recently.

Badminton 1988

Photo by Joan - probably

I recall some lovely holidays with them in Dorset, Montgomery, Mid-Wales and then in Rutland. Gordon was on a walking holiday in Austria with a friend of his and so while he was away Margaret came with us to Rutland. Margaret and I spent some time on Rutland Water on a boat, but while we had an interesting commentary from the captain, it was annoyingly almost totally drowned out by some members of a coach party who talked incessantly throughout – and wouldn't take a hint.

We then had an extremely interesting day in Stamford, where the Town Guide took us around all the buildings of interest. He then showed us a lovely olde worlde café with lots of chintz, where we finished a lovely day with a very nice tea.

My last memory of Margaret is a sad one – we had returned from a holiday and she and I had gone to Waitrose to do some shopping and Margaret asked to be dropped at Boots on Church Street. I remember quite clearly her standing on the steps of Boots and giving me a little wave.

Well, tragically the next morning Gordon came round at about 7 o'clock to say that Margaret was ill. We rang for an ambulance immediately and went over to their house. Joan went up to see Margaret and I waited in the lane to show the ambulance where to go. Sadly despite the fact that the medics were there very quickly there was nothing they could do…..

Joan with Honey and
Don & Pat Cairns
at Carew Castle in June 1999

Taken by Jo outside Carew Mill with the castle in background

The Hills have always been on our doorstep of course, but we've never taken them for granted or forgotten them – and the dogs always enjoyed them too!

The Beacon

Rosie and Jo on Midsummer Hill

Photo by Joan

In 1989 we drove south to Penhow, near Chepstow in Monmouthshire, for the day.

In Penhow is a Norman castle which is still lived in, but we were able to go in and look around. It was turned into a house hundreds of years ago and is lovely little place – but we were told it is haunted…

Near to it is the church of St. John the Baptist. It's supposed to be as old as the castle, and we read that it was built in 1290, so Joan thought that made sense.

Above, Penhow Castle

Left, sitting outside St.John's church.

Photos by Joan

It was a really lovely day and we had a drink and lunch in the old coaching inn there, the Rock & Fountain Inn.

The next year we went down to Exmouth with Barbara, in 1990.

Looking at the pictures now, it seems that we must have always had lovely weather back then, but I suppose we only took photos on good days!

Closer to home, we visited Chirk, near Wrexham, where the Llangollen Canal crosses very high over the River Dee with the Pontcysyllte aqueduct. I walked a little way along the towpath with the two dachs. The canal in an iron trough – but there's only a thin railing between you and a 130ft drop – and nothing at all on the other side!   Joan didn't want to come....

Photo by Joan

However, I came back after only getting half way along there because the dogs kept sticking their heads through the railings and I was scared of them falling through and dangling over the great drop on the ends of their leads.... So I came back.

But then we went down to walk along underneath by the river and from there it all looked even more impressive.

We certainly did have some good days, but so many of my good friends have gone now. Because I knew them all for so long, I suppose that's why I'm sometimes asked to say a few words at the end. Cath recalls that I did it at Rene's funeral too.

"Joan and Jo always called my mum Renie, whereas her name was just Rene. But Jo has a real talent for all sorts of things and she made a wonderful job of Mum's eulogy. Later she also did the same at the funeral of Charlie Williams." (See Appx. 3)

Time Well Spent

We spent time throughout 1980s and '90s fundraising with the Malvern Hills Support Group for St. Michaels Hospice, based in Bartestree, which is a very worthwhile charity which started back in the 1970s. It cares for people suffering from terminal illnesses, as well as supporting their families. We helped, together with friends, with their activities and took along stuff for their stalls – plants, cakes, fruit, that sort of stuff. We also organised a range of fund raising activities such as Coffee Mornings and Evenings over the years. We enjoyed it, met lots of nice people – and we did help the Hospice I think.

Press photo

Pat Cox, Jo, Log and Joan received Gold Awards for 15 years' service.
Diana Dawes (far right) received a Silver Award for 10 years.

In fact, we were even given Long Service Awards, presented by the Hospice Chief Executive, Mr. Walter Brooks.

"Without people like them we wouldn't survive" he said at the ceremony. *"Only 14% of our income comes from the NHS. The rest comes from voluntary sources."*

Reading for the blind was something else I did for several years in the 1990s, which I found very interesting and worthwhile. It involved going into town to recording sessions once a month and I soon got the hang of it all. We were expected to choose our own material and I always tried to find an interesting piece - something that I had read that amused me, or I thought was particularly interesting. At that time I regularly took a small magazine called *The Dalesman* and I often found stories in there which were very amusing.

I've already mentioned that in 1999 we took part in quite big fund-raising event in aid of the local churches – the Worcester, Dudley & District Historic Churches Trust Sponsored Ride. Now, as I've already said, I could and did ride a bicycle when I was younger, but I'd not really done much of it since the end of the war. So getting back on again was something of a challenge – but it's nothing like getting back onto a horse, so I did it alright. Mind you, I did have a bit of help and support from Gill Ferris, who is good at riding a bike. She lent me her 'Giant' mountain bike and I got along well enough. We visited the churches at Hanley Swan, Poolbrook, Madresfield, Welland and of course Guarlford.

Gill Ferris, Jo, Liz Tiball, Don Hill and Pauline Cooper at the start, at Guarlford.

Gill, Liz and Jo
at just one of the many churches they visited

144

Visitations

Talking of Gill, we used to visit Joan's nephew John and his wife Gill when they lived not too far away in Hartlebury, when John worked at Stourport-on-Severn High School. While they lived there in the 1980s, they had two children, Toby and Lindsay.

Then because of John's job they moved to Tamworth, which is a quite a bit further away and in the town, but we visited them there too.

Jo outside 4 Brunel Close, in Tamworth. J&J's VW and J&G's 2CV on the drive.

Photo by John

Coffee time at Tamworth. Toby has Katy on his lap, but Joan was probably dragged off somewhere by Lindsay, as she always specially liked Joan.

Photo by Gill

In 1991 they moved all the way up to Lancaster, because John had got a job as a college lecturer there. They lived in a small flat on campus, so we stayed in a B&B nearby which could take dogs.

On top of a nearby hill is a lovely big park, Williamson's Park, and so we took the dogs for a walk there.

Gill, Jo and Joan in front of the Williamson Memorial.

Photo by John

145

Forever A Farmer

Throughout this time, there were still always things to be done in the paddocks or in the garden of course.

*Jo, Iris, Bruce and Colin
Haymaking.*

*Jo on the
tractor,
followed by
Iris*

I was retired, but still pretty fit I think, I could do most of it myself most of the time, anyway, although I left hefting the bales to others!

I've always been pretty lucky health-wise, apart from accidents, which I've had too many of over the years. But then, I suppose that's because I could never have done with just a desk job, trapped in an office all day, which would have been safer for me perhaps, but I'm quite certain I'd not have been like I am now if I'd been deskbound all my life......

A long the length of the back paddock there was a fence and we thought that we could plant a hedge there, which would be better than wire fencing. It was a good idea, but then it got a bit carried away…

Jo and Lisa the Munsterlander, right at the start of planting what turned out to be a long, narrow copse

Press photo

The nursery always stocked Christmas trees in season, but there were usually some left over, which we had previously just burned. However, some of them had roots, so this time we planted them along the boundary, together with various saplings and shrubs that we couldn't sell in the nursery. It was turning into a long, narrow copse and would obviously provide shelter for wildlife.

Anyway, the press got to hear about this and they must have been short of any real news at the time because the Malvern Gazette sent a reporter and a photographer along to get a story out of it! Conservation and 'greening the countryside' was all the rage just then, so I suppose that we had (briefly) come back into fashion?

In time, the copse has developed well and no longer looks so much like a man-made plantation. I don't really know what wildlife lives there, but it must help. We sold the land some time ago, and so the copse as well, and a neighbour farms it now with crops and sheep in rotation, but I still take the dog for a walk there every day and it makes a nice walk with friends.

Jo, Di and Dorothy

Foot and Mouth Disease

We had a bad case of foot & mouth in this country in 1967. It started not far away in Shropshire and ended up with over 400,000 cattle being slaughtered and burned! At the time I was in the Car Service, but Joan and I still had a few beef cattle on the farm. Of course, everything was shut down to stop it spreading and so at Grange Farm we survived without any losses, thank god.

And then it happened all over again in 2001. By then we no longer had cattle, nothing cloven-hooved at all, so it didn't affect us directly. However, we were still part of the local farming community which <u>was</u> seriously affected, so we did what we could to help.

Merial Bennett agreed to fill in some of the details and she describes how she was helped once again by Jo:

"During the foot & mouth outbreak in 2001, I was unexpectedly left caring for a flock of sheep from the Welsh hills, all heavily in lamb, which should have been taken back to their home farm to lamb. However, due to the Livestock Movement Restriction, we were not permitted to do so and they had to remain at my already overcrowded little holding.

Once again Jo came to the rescue, offering her experienced assistance when looking round all the expectant flock, and later checking on the youngsters once lambing was under way.

Jo's help there was an absolute godsend as there were never enough hours in the day for all the extra work which Francis, my husband, and I were forced to undertake."

Jo, Merial & Francis at their farm

149

Rosemary McCulloch also remembers this time, with a little help from her diaries and back copies of the Malvern Gazette:

"When Foot & Mouth broke out again in 2001, the local churches wanted to do something practical to help the farming community and so the ARC* Addington Fund was founded. The main point was to help struggling farmers and anyone involved in farming - for example, the people who maintained the agricultural machinery.

So Jo led us in forming the Guarlford & District Farmers' Support Group. *The first event, I think, was a Coffee Morning held in the gardens of Grange Farm on Thursday 5th July 2001, which raised the astounding sum of £511."*

"Then came the ambitious Farmers' Supper in the Village Hall on October 26th. The plan was to provide a supper of a main course of beef casserole and mashed potatoes, followed by apple pie & ice-cream, ending with cheeses & biscuits. So many events were being cancelled that Jo thought farmers and other country people deserved an evening out - so tickets were just £6.

We wrote letters to all the Malvern Supermarkets, asking for help (i.e. free food!) and Jo & I went to collect meat from Waitrose, Malvern Country Meals, and P. Phipps of Hanley Swan. All the vegetables were given to us by Safeway, a large spread of English cheeses came from Somerfield, with the biscuits given by the Hanley Swan Post Office & Stores. Bennetts Dairies came up trumps with lots of delicious ice-cream, and Pat Robinson got apple pies from Kay's canteen.

I can't recall all the details, but we seem also to have had a raffle, tombola and an auction on the night. Jo was amazing every time as she and others went to the local shops asking for prizes. Anyway, the result was that various ladies made beef casseroles and pots of mashed potatoes, everyone enjoyed a very sociable evening and a massive £1,178 was raised.

I have a note in my diary for 13th November 2001 that Mrs Berrington of Little Malvern Court arranged that we should receive a further £1,000 to add to our appeal from a charity that she knew.

Finally I see that in the following Spring we held a Coffee Morning on Saturday 6th April 2002 in the Playroom of Madresfield Court (by kind permission of Lady Morrison). We charged £1 to include coffee, and there were stalls selling cakes, produce, crafts and a raffle. I think we were all very surprised when we realised that we had made £345.50. People were very generous, and Jo started it all."

Well yes, it was certainly an awful time for the farmers all over the country, and so we did what we could. The pictures on the TV of all the fires up in Cumbria were terrible – John remembers driving up the M6, from Lancaster to Carlisle, and seeing and smelling some of the fires. Most distressing.

And little were we to know it would all happen again in 2007 – although it didn't get to this area that time, thank goodness.

---

* **ARC** The Arthur Rank Centre, the rural resource unit for the churches in England. Canon Richard Addington inspired the original Addington Fund in East Anglia.

The Pond

We had always wanted a 'water feature' - or a duck pond as some of our 'friends' called it. So in 1982 we actually did it. The bit of lawn behind the tack-shed wasn't being used really, so that's were we chose to dig it.

A friend came round with a big yellow JCB digger and made short work of it!

The Hole
In the background can be seen our old tack-shed, now long gone as it's now Nursery Land.

A very large plastic lining was put in and then slabs laid around it.
It's all well overgrown now, so most of that can't be seen any more, but that's how it was.

Jo and Toby found that the new pond was also ideal for sailing small boats!

Before long we realised that the pond was yet another part of our gardens that needed constant maintenance – every few years or so it needed draining and 'weeding' as it quickly became overgrown. In 2006 it badly needed doing again so I decided to improve things a bit by converting some of it into 'wetland'.

One day, when I was working on it, I tripped and fell in. When I'd got myself out, Joan was laughing her head off and said that I looked like the *Creature From The Deep*…. !

She made me strip off in the back porch before having a warm shower.

However, it still gets overgrown rather quickly…

Meanwhile, our garden was going rampant too…..

Birthdays and Christmases

On one occasion I had planned a surprise party for Joan's birthday, and our friends were each bringing something to eat. Well, people were due to arrive at about 7.30 - and at 6.30 Joan decided to wash her hair!

"You haven't got time for that! They'll be here soon!" I said, beginning to panic a bit.

"Oh, it won't take long, just a quick wash......" and she went off to the bathroom and started washing her hair! Then it needed drying – and I tried to speed things up by turning the drier up a bit, but as soon as I did that, Joan turned it back down again. Well, in the end, she was just about decent when the first of them arrived – but it was quite a game hurrying her on for the past hour.

Joan had her 80th birthday in 1998 and so there was to be a family gathering at Grange Farm to celebrate it. Typically, Joan didn't want to make a fuss of it - but everybody else did, and lots of people arrived in the morning of her birthday, to all go out to the pub for a Birthday Lunch.

Mo, Toby, Ian, John, Rosie & Honey, Joan, Colin,
Fiona, Lindsay, Gill & Meg

Photo by Jo

Naturally it was mostly Joan's family there, so we had Joan's brother Colin down from Stafford; her nephew Ian, with his wife Mo and daughter Fiona from Derby; her nephew John, with his wife Gill and son Toby and daughter Lindsay from Lancaster; and Rosie was there too.

We did have a bit of a slap-up meal - and even managed tea in the garden later on.

I think Joan enjoyed it – certainly she liked having all the friends and family around.

153

And then in 2003 I reached the age of 80, so Joan and I were able to have enjoyed each other's 80th birthdays. Mine was a very special do for me because Gill had organised for me to drive a big lorry once again! I've said a bit about that in Chapter 10, where there's a picture of me up in the cab of a very big lorry. I kept my end up, didn't make a mess of it and at the end I was complemented by the Instructor, which was very nice.

We had a little party too and then in the evening some of us went out for a meal so, all in all, it really was good birthday for me.

Joan's 86th birthday was coming up in 2005 and I thought I'd plan an especially good day out for her - with a trip in a landau. I had arranged for us to go to the Plough & Harrow at about 11.30, to surprise Joan with the horse and carriage waiting for her there.

So on the morning of her birthday, I casually mentioned that we'd be meeting up with some friends for a drink at the Plough, but Joan said that I should go on my own as she was not feeling so good and would probably go back to bed!
Well, what was I to do? She couldn't be persuaded in any usual way, so I just had to tell her what had been planned…. She did of course rise to the occasion and it all turned out alright, but it was a bit of a tense moment for me, I can tell you!

We arrived at the Plough, where there were some of our friends already waiting for us, and so Joan was toasted by Merial and all of us with champagne.

Joan was of course delighted with her treat – she was well dressed for the occasion and looking good, with a big smile on her face throughout. The ride was around the area, stopping back at Grange Farm for a change of passengers – not Joan of course, she stayed put!

A change of passengers at the Farm – Jo and Gill ride with Joan

Fortunately we were blessed with lovely weather – that could have made all the difference!

The finish of the Ride back at the Plough & Harrow – with more champagne!

And the food prepared by Gill for afterwards was, of course, as always, very good.

Joan's Birthday Lunch, complete with cards (and a hopeful dog underneath the table)

"I love to cook with a good wine.   Sometimes I even put some into the food."

Anon

Back in Chapter 7 I talked about our Christmases at Guarlford, and I don't think we ever had a duff one really – plenty of friends and plenty of drinks make sure it all goes well.

We'd always have a traditional meal at home of course, but when friends or family turned up beforehand, often we'd go out for a meal in the pub.

Jo, Ian, Colin, John and Joan at the Duke of York, in 1999

I like the way that Christmas is celebrated in the countryside – but I'm sure it's all very different in the city!

Christmas Fair outside Hanley Swan Village Stores

By way of something of a contrast, in 2010 I expected to spend Christmas Day at home and alone, but then I asked John what he was doing over Christmas and he said he'd like to spend it with me here, so that was alright. He said that he could cook the veg if I looked after the turkey, and of course I could. Anyway, after he'd gone back up north again, planning to come back here just before Christmas Eve, I 'phoned him up just to check that he'd not had second thoughts or anything... He said he was looking forward to it, so I dropped my bombshell on him:

"Well, I hope you don't mind, John, but there'll be three of us for dinner."

"What? That's not what I agreed to! Who is it, anyway?" He didn't sound keen – I expect he thought we'd be talking about hunting, shooting and fishing all through the meal, or something.

"Well, it's the Vicar." He was a little bit surprised about that. Well, a lot surprised I suppose. I explained that Sue Irwin would be in the area, having done the Christmas Day services in the local churches and so would appreciate a break and something to eat.

In the end it all went very well, and the vegetables were not too bad after all! John and I had a few cooks' tipples, but Sue didn't want much, because she'd already had plenty of free, holy wine in church... She didn't have a cup of tea afterwards either, as she doesn't like tea – which greatly disappointed John, because that meant that he couldn't come out with:

"More tea, Vicar?"

Sue and Jo about to tuck into the Christmas Pud

Photo by John

157

Life Goes On

In between special days, like birthdays and whatever, life goes on of course and there's always jobs to be done, people to visit, events to go to and whiskey to be tasted.....

We did have a whiskey tasting session at the Mount Pleasant which was all very interesting I must say. Some of them were very nice indeed, although I definitely prefer the peaty ones. But we were told that one of them was *"something a bit special......"*, - but when we tried it, it was absolutely AWFUL! One tiny sip was enough for me and I don't remember anyone who liked it – and yet it was around £35 a bottle!

Joan and Jo,
together with Margaret Earp,
near Montgomery

When I can, and when the weather is good enough, I still like to turn up at a local Meet.

Jo, Chris and Emma at Madresfield in 1998

I even had a share in a racehorse once again, for a while anyway. I'd go across to the stables to see how things were shaping up, which was all very interesting and sociable too. In the end he went lame, so couldn't race and was given to a girl to ride. So that came to an end for me.

In October 2005 I had a go at the I.A.M.'s Advanced Driving Test, just for the hell of it I suppose. And I passed!

So, I am now a Member of the Institute of Advanced Motorists, which also helps with my insurance premiums. (See Appx. 9)

In the late 1990s, my cousins Pat and David decided to use their birthday as a reason for a family get-together. We all met at the Chateau Impney, in Droitwich, and we had a lovely lunch.

Jo, Joan, Maggie (my cousin), Eddy (her husband), Shaun (my second cousin) and his wife, and Steven (my third cousin) and his wife

There are many other occasions I can recall were when we just met up with friends, some of whom are no longer with us – but definitely worth remembering!

Peggy having a joke with Bella and Mac.

Dachs Katie & Tansie under the table

Thankfully, however, there are still a few of 'em left!

159

Rosie, Di, Jo and Gill

*Jo with her cousin Pat Cairns
and Don, in 2001*

There were so many little occasions that were enjoyable at the time, so many people that were good company in lots of ways – I can't remember them all and certainly there's not room here for all the hundreds of pictures in the albums that Joan kept – all in order and with titles and notes. Not only that but she kept her diary every day for the whole of her life – there's three shelves of them in the middle room! And then she was frequently reading about and making notes about local history – but thankfully it has all been put together and used well by the Guarlford History Group, in the book '*The Guarlford Story*', which they published in 2005. We were very pleased to see Joan credited with all her work at the launch of the book – and she was very pleased too, naturally.

Of course, sadly the biggest recent event, or change, in my life was when I lost my partner and lifetime friend, Joan. She was becoming very frail by about 2005 or '06 - but, typically of Joan, she wouldn't give in to it and kept going as long as she possibly could.

However, here I'll choose to pass over what was a very difficult time, and Joan finally left us, in her sleep, on 2nd May, 2007.

I even know about what time it was too, because I heard her calling me…

Merial and Gill were here that night and I went to her room, where Merial was with her, but she had gone.

Merial said that she'd definitely not heard Joan calling out to me, but I know that she did. Somehow.

Joan was taken to St.Mary's Church by horse, naturally.

Photos by John

Joan's gravestone

**LOVING MEMORIES
OF
JOAN BRADSHAW
1918 – 2007**

**DEEP PEACE OF THE QUIET
EARTH TO YOU**

161

Looking Back

All in all, Joan and I have led a very active life really when I look in her diary. It was a 'day-to-day' diary so it's all there - and I really don't know how we did it all. We were always off somewhere. We went to parties there and we had barbeques here and, I don't know, we went doing this and doing that and doing the other – almost every week! We went to all the shows, The Royal, The Three Counties and other events and we went racing too. We used to go down to Devon and up to Northumberland and people used to say *"You're never at home!"* I must say that, looking at Joan's diaries, it doesn't look as though we were at home many weekends at all!

Oh, we worked very hard and I suppose we played very hard, but we were young and if that's what you can do, why not? I must admit we went on doing it until we were quite, quite old and well retired. Well into our retirement we still went here, there and everywhere together. I advise everyone to do it, do what you can while you can, that was our philosophy of life. So I still do if I can, although I'm getting a little bit creaky now I suppose. However, my doctor has finally figured out just what my problem is: *"You've got the mind of a 30 year old in the body of an 80 year old....."*

Maybe so, but that's much better than having it other way round!

Jo and Lucy in the Snug at The Three Kings, May 2012

Photo by John

Appendix 1

LIONESS

August 2009

LIONESS
Journal of the WRAC Association
Vol.LXXXV No.2 2011

MEMORIES OF WARTIME SERVICE
Jo Newell

Whilst delivering milk in Worcester one day I saw a convoy of lorries going through – driven by girls! I thought "Ah that is for me". So off I went to the recruiting office to join up. I was 17 and keen but they said "You are too young, but we will in touch with you when you are 18". Anyway come April and on my birthday I was watching the post but still nothing came. Eventually in May it came and it gave me a week to get ready and go. My father nearly had a fit and so did my mother, but anyway they accepted the fact that I wanted to go and so off I went.

I joined up and volunteered as a river in the Pioneer Corps, Transport Section. I went to Derring Lines in Brecon where I had 6 weeks of sheer misery really. We had a lot of square bashing, blisters on our heels, and we had starched collars which gave you blisters on your neck. It was June and it was really hot and we were taken on route marches and the food awful and we all had our jabs which were ditto and were all very glad to move away from there. From there I went up to Chilwell near Nottingham. We were sent on a course of advanced driving, learning how to drive big lorries and all different sorts of vehicles which were very difficult for us. We drove all round the Nottingham countryside, stopping and having a cup of coffee in the middle of the morning and we took our own packed lunch. We had to take a test which we all passed and then we were posted.

I was fortunate enough to be posted to Shrewsbury and went into private billets there, but it was not so great really as I was on my own with two old ladies, one of whom appeared to me to be ancient! We were doing convoy duty which involved picking up lorries from factories all over the country and taking them to various depots and we were away for at least two nights on some details. These two dear old ladies knew the Army rules were that I was supposed to be in by 10 o'clock every night and they could not understand when I was not in at 10 o'clock every night when I was on duty. Also they certainly could not understand me having to get up at 5 o'clock and have my breakfast! It was very difficult for them and these two old ladies must have wondered what had hit them. Anyway I did not stay there long; obviously they could not accept it at all. I then went to stay with a family where the husband was in the RAF and there were 5 children and it was such a complete contrast; so free and easy and you could come and go as you pleased.

By the time I had got to Shrewsbury I had been initiated into the do's and don'ts of Army life very quickly but there was more to come. We three were the first new recruits they had had and they were great. There was not one of them that I could say was snooty or snobbish in any way. Very loyal to each other, very loyal and great fun – we laughed most of the time. Anyway we used to go to the Birmingham factories and pick up trucks and then we used to go all the way down to Dagenham and pick up Fords. We had to quickly get used to lots of different set ups because you would be driving something different every day. Back in Harlscote we used to drive some of the big tanks and put them on the

Getting to know the vehicles we were to drive

trains. We used to drive them up to the railway station, making a right mess of the roads, and on into the goods yards. We also used to take Bren gun carriers and something called a Dragon, which was bigger than a Bren but steered by two levers. You had a week on Depot duty where you did this sort of thing and then you got trucks ready for convoy that were going out the next day. Then you'd be out for about 6 weeks and then have another week in.

We saw lots of Britain on those times. We went to all the dock towns of course; Liverpool, Portsmouth, Swansea, Southampton. That was the job really, just back and forwards all over England all the time. There were incidents. I should explain that for the first two years most of the trucks we drove were completely open. There was no protection for the driver, no hood, no anything. There was a little postage stamp windscreen but it did not help much. We had one quite tough trip to Scotland. We had set off quite early in the morning and there were abut 30 of us I think. It was pouring with rain and we had gone about half a mile when my truck boiled. It had completely run out of water. So down on the wet road I had to get and turn the bottom tap off. Later we were sitting having fish and chips and somebody said "look out of the window". I have never before or since seen such big snow flakes, they were like saucers and by the time we got back the snow on my seat was about 6 inches deep! We were supposed to be going to Carlisle that night. Anyway after a lot of getting stuck and digging out and sliding and slithering we eventually got as far as Kendal. Six of us were put up in the Mason's Arms and we were glad just to sit there with a whiskey! The next day was a day of dig out, get stuck, dig out, get stuck, dig out. We left Kendal about eleven in the morning and I personally got there about ten o'clock at night, frozen. However we did get to Glasgow eventually with the majority of the vehicles intact.

We also used to go to the Birmingham factories and pick up trucks and also all the way to Dagenham and pick up Fords. We had to quickly get used to lots of different set ups because you would be driving something different every day. Sometimes the gear boxes were 1,2,3,4,R and sometimes 4,3,2,1,R or even R,1,2,3,4.

At the end of the war, believe it or not, I very nearly volunteered to stay on because, in reality, I loved the life in the Army. Unfortunately my father had a heart attack and so I had to go home to help.

Appendix 2

TRACTOR
August 2009

Words Pete Henshaw
Pictures Newell & Bradshaw families

Worcestershire memories

Charlie Williams and Jo Newell today, still living in the same Shropshire village.

Jo Newell and Charlie Williams both farmed near the village of Guarlford, just outside Malvern, and recall life back in the 40s and 50s.

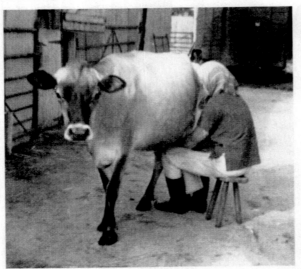

Before milking machines... Joan hand milking in the yard at Grange Farm.

Jo Newell and Charlie Williams loved horses, and both of them saw Shropshire farming transform from horse to tractor power in the 40s and 50s.

Jo has had what you might call an interesting life. At the age of 18, she volunteered for war service driving new lorries from factories to docks. Her memoirs have tales of driving over Shap Fell in the middle of winter with no cab, open to the elements.

That army experience was put to good use after the war, when she dealt with all types of wagons, tractors and trailers.

A farmer at heart

Her first car was a 1929 Riley 9 Lynx, which she and partner Joan Bradshaw used for all sorts of farm jobs, carrying bales of hay, piglets and lambs, pulling hen houses across the fields, even towing trailers full of calves to market when the lorry wasn't available. On occasion, it would also whizz she and Joan up to London to see a show in the West End. The Riley eventually made way for a series of SWB Land Rovers, and Jo gained her Institute of Advanced Motorists qualification at the age of 80. More recently, she spent her birthday driving a 16-wheeler truck.

But at heart, Jo was a farmer and horsewoman and she explained how it all started: "I went to my uncle's farm when I was a kid, I loved horses and it was all I wanted to do – be with horses on a farm. When I came out of the army at the end of the war, I got a job with a farmer who did pigs and poultry, and I later went to work for Tolley. He had a small mixed farm – 25 cows, about 40 sheep, some pigs, Christmas turkey, and the horses of course...you couldn't make a living out of that now.

Horses remained Jo's first love. She also rode motorbikes...

It looks picturesque, but hay making and threshing was hard work.

An early love of horses stayed with Joan for life.

"I met Joan Bradshaw, who shared my love of horses, and we had a great time there, getting the horses fit. The sheep had to be fed in the winter, and lambed in the spring – they were lambed outdoors then – and I spent many a night cold and wet outside. It was much better when we started lambing indoors. I only sheared a sheep once, it was damn hard work!

"We milked by hand, into a bucket, and had to start at 5am because they came to collect it at seven. Later we had a milking machine, but on very cold mornings – we used to get proper frosts then – the pulsators would freeze up. You'd have to take them up to the farmhouse and put them in the oven to thaw out! The diesel engine for our milking machine didn't have electric start and had to be swung into life. It could be a pig on cold mornings. You don't know what a joy it was when we went over to an electric machine and you just had to press a button.

Work hard, play hard

"We worked hard, but we played hard too. In the winter, you couldn't work in the evenings so that's when your social life was. We'd go and have dinner with friends or go down to the pub. The pub stayed open late, because sometimes we'd be hay making until 10 o'clock at night then go and have a few beers. In the country, nobody cared about opening times.

"Joan went to agricultural college, but it was so different then, because girls weren't supposed to

have anything to do with cattle. She was allowed to learn about poultry, but she would sneak into the cattle lectures as well. I didn't go to college, but it was amazing how much I picked up as a kid, because I spent a lot of time on the farm.

"We built hay ricks after the binder had gone round, and that was a horrible job. You had to wear long sleeves or you'd get scratched to bits. You'd leave them three weeks or so to dry out. Life was much more leisurely then. There would be three or four of you on hay making, and the farmer's wife would bring down tea and cakes, and there'd be a lot of banter and leg-pulling, you know. There was always somebody to talk to, someone hedging or ditching. These days farmers work on their own, and seem to be on the tractor all day. It must be very boring, and I think that's why a lot of farmers feel isolated now.

"Everything was done by horses, until Tolley bought his first tractor, a Fordson, in 1948, the one with the wide wings. He learnt about machinery as he went along. Then he bought a baler, a stationary one – the bales weighed a ton and it was still hard work but then, joy of joys, we had the first pick-up baler, I think it was a Bamford. It kept going wrong at first, with the knotter that tied the bales up, and we'd have to shake the hay out and rebale it, but eventually it was sorted out. It was wonderful, with an elevator taking bales onto the wagon, which saved a lot of hard work.

"The transition to machinery was quite slow in those days, because a lot of farmers resisted tractors. It was often a son who would say, 'Come on dad, let's buy a tractor'. And when they did begin to change, it had a sad side. At Stow Horse Fair, there would be hundreds of heavy horses waiting to go to slaughter, which was heartbreaking. Looking back, I don't know how some of the farmers did it. You have a relationship with a horse you see – you don't get that with a tractor.

"I did drive the tractors, spent hours and hours on them, and it was very boring. And the Fordson had no brakes! If you pressed the clutch pedal right down, it was supposed to operate the brake, but it didn't. I was coming back with a load of corn on the trailer one day, down a steep hill, and couldn't stop. There was a chap standing on the tractor with me and we managed to pull up by the Blue Bell, so we went in for a drink to recover!

Half-leg horse

"Later, Joan's parents became ill, so she and I came back to farm here. Old Tolley was quite good, he would lend us tractors, but we had a horse as well. A horse with a float was very useful for odd jobs, like foddering and fencing. A lot of people kept what we called a half-leg horse – heavier than a cob but lighter than a shire. You could ride them or drive them, and a lot of farmers had one of those and a tractor. In lots of ways, the horse was cheaper, and they last longer! ↄ

XV

"Eventually we did buy a Fergie, which was a fantastic little tractor. We used that to make silage, with a buckrake on it – when that was loaded, you'd come down the road with your front wheels off the ground! You'd get locked up if you did that now, but nobody took much notice then. Life was much easier, and there was less traffic on the roads. My favourite tractor, though, was the Dexta – so small and handy.

"Tolly had a Fordson Major as well, a great high thing, and it was dangerous because it was top heavy. I was foddering the cattle one day, and his daughter was helping me – she was about 10 – and I set her on driving the tractor, because you did that with kids then, when they were big enough. I was on top of the trailer, forking the hay out, looked up and we were heading straight for the brook. I shouted, but she had frozen, so I had to jump off the trailer, run alongside and jump onto this high tractor. I grabbed the steering wheel, and I think we missed the brook by two or three feet!'

Horseman, not tractorman

Charlie Williams was born in 1923, and has clear memories of just how hard farming was in the 1930s. "It was really terrible. Corn was less than £5 a ton, and they'd get half a ton per acre. After paying for the land, they'd be left with only about 15 bob to pay for the seed and for someone to plant it and work it. They couldn't afford even to pay the women to dig up the docks and the thistles, so it all went wild. Farmers were often in debt. In came the Canadian wheat, the New Zealand butter and the Danish bacon, Argentine meat. Terrible it was. Farms were going bust left right and centre, and I saw farmers at market with tears running down their cheeks.

"During the war the subsidies came in, and we were busy, and after the war it all changed again. The little Fergie tractor was around, and chaps didn't want to walk after horses any more, so the horses went for slaughter – didn't matter if they were two or 25-year-old, they all went. It was wicked. I was the last man to cut corn and plough with horses in this village. Mind you, it was good in

Joan and a young John Bradshaw enjoy a ride in the cart.

a way that they went, because some of the horses were badly treated – collar and hay for breakfast, gateposts and hay for dinner, we used to say.

"We took care in training the horses. You'd bring one in at two years old and hook him up to some weight, a sleeper or something, to get him used to it. Otherwise he could turn into a gibber, a horse that wouldn't work. Then you'd try him on the plough, as part of a team, for just an hour, and keep on extending it until he could do a day. At four years old you'd try him on the binder, with a few steadier horses to go with him. By five years old, you could do anything with him.

"When folk used to come and buy horses, the corporations and the brewers wanted good-looking beasts, but the timber folk weren't bothered how ugly they were so long as they could work. A dealer would watch the horse walk, leave him in the yard to see if he would wait quietly, then wave a handkerchief in front of his eyes. If the horse could do all that, he might fetch 50 guineas.

"Tractors didn't always work as well as horses. It was a wet autumn, 1946, and I took two horses to plough potatoes out for a farmer, sowed corn and harrowed. They couldn't use the tractors you see, because it was too wet. I did drive a tractor once, but a tree bough flicked over the exhaust and hit me in the face, and I was shouting 'Whoa!' Oh no, I couldn't get on with tractors.

Plane crash

"I nearly met my Waterloo one Saturday in April 1944. I was working in the rick yard here when I heard this plane come over low. He took the tops of the trees off and hit the ground. I ran up there, and found an airman hiding behind the crab apple tree. I didn't know if he was English or German at first. His shoulder was all broken, and he said the pilot was still in the plane but he was done for.

"I ran over to the plane, and the pilot was still sat there, burning but unconscious, so I put my arms under his shoulders and pulled him out, parachute and all. I dragged him out about a dozen yards and the cannon shells started exploding. They had just refuelled in Bristol so the plane was full of fuel as well. I managed to get him into the ditch; the Americans were nearby, and they took him to hospital. Nine months later the pilot and his wife came to see me, and later they moved to Australia. They'd always send me a Christmas card, and a few years ago his son came over. I got a medal for saving him, had to go to Buckingham Palace for that.

"By the time the war ended, I was working on my own. Then the combines came in as well as the tractors, and they didn't want the labour. The seven farms round here, six dairy and one with hops and vegetables, employed 28 men between them, plus women. Not any more – now it's just one bloke on one farm working the whole lot.

"I was offered a lot of money for my five acres a few years ago, but I wouldn't take it. What's the use of money? You can only eat one steak, only drive one car and only cuddle one woman, and if you want more you're a greedy bugger! That's what I told 'em."

Thanks to John Bradshaw for his help with this article. ∎

Joan, here in that 1929 Riley 9, learnt to drive at a young age.

xvi

Appendix 3
Jo's TRIBUTE TO CHARLIE WILLIAMS

I first knew Charlie in about 1949, but our first meeting was not very auspicious. Joan Bradshaw and I were riding two very fit point-to-pointers up the Guarlford Common, when Charlie came up behind us driving a pony and trap quite quickly. Now for some reason, some ridden horses dislike driven horses coming up behind them and our two did take exception to it. They whipped round and generally played up and so we had some rather strong words with Charlie, undoubtedly containing the odd rude word. But Charlie just laughed and said: *"You'll be all right kid."*

But as we got to know Charlie, dealing with sheep and horses, he became a good friend. One night we were struggling to lamb a ewe at about two in the morning. She had three lambs in a right tangle and we just couldn't get them, so I went to fetch Charlie. I threw some gravel up to the bedroom window. Charlie's head appeared and I told him the trouble.
"Hang on kid!" he said and seconds later he came out through the door doing his buttons up. After a long struggle we got three live lambs out.
Charlie was a born stockman and so gentle with the sheep. I believe farmers used to turn up on his doorstep with a ewe in the back of a Land-Rover to get Charlie to lamb the ewe.

The first inkling we had that Charlie and Do were courting was when we were driving over Sherrards Green Common and there were Charlie and Doreen having a cuddle under one of the trees. Of course we shouted and hollered and blew the horn, all laughing our heads off.
Then came the wedding day. They left the church in a smart pony and trap – what else? – and on the back of the trap was: *'Done Roaming'*.
On one occasion, rather later on, we were driving past Charlie's and he came out of the gate being chased by Do with a carving knife. We stopped and cheered her on and when they couldn't run any more we were all laughing too much to move.

Then of course came their family and I think you'll all agree they made a pretty good job of it. I clearly recall Jackie's wedding. Firstly the shafts broke on the dray and they had to get another set –and that one was 100 years old! Then the video wouldn't work. Her petticoat got caught up in the dray. In church a pedestal fell over and to cap it all, when she got to the Reception, a gust of wind took her headdress off over the Club! In spite of all that it was a lovely day for everyone.

But of course Charlie's great pride and joy was his horses. The pleasure they gave him was beyond measure. They really were his life. Whenever we went to see Charlie or we went by, we had to go and see the horses and his thoroughbred stallion, 'Paddy', who was always brought out to be admired, and a super horse he was too.
He also had one called 'Flower' who did logging, and there was 'Bluebell' who took him to church to be married and later took his son Dick to be christened.
The Shires were 'Cotswold Grey King', called 'Tom'; 'Whitney Majestic', called 'Click', as well as 'Leystone Quicksilver'. And then there was 'Judy', who he said had a bit of Clydsdale in her.
I don't think anyone realises the hard work that goes on behind the scenes to result in the spectacle of Shires in their harness. One night I called to see Charlie, and he and Do had got all the tack all laid out across the floor, cleaning all the beautiful brasses and leatherwork.

Joan and I bought a filly foal from Charlie and so he brought her down loose behind the mare at about 6 o'clock one morning and she turned out to be a real pet. She was more like a dog than a horse. When we were cleaning out her stable she would walk out and wander around the yard and come up and give you a nudge for a tit-bit. One day I was getting hay out of the barn and she came wandering down the drive and I said *"And where do you think you're going to?"* but she just gave me a look and went on - and then simply jumped the gate out onto the road! I ran out in to the road after her, afraid she would just take off, but she just stood there and then followed me back in as though nothing had happened.

She bred two foals, one a colt, who was born in the early hours out in the field, when just then a fox ran across the field. So as he was by 'Lord Fox', we called him 'Charlie Fox'.

When the filly was about four months old, the mare had a bad attack of colic and you have to walk them round and round and stop them lying down. After about an hour we were getting worn out and so I fetched Charlie. We spent the whole night trying to stop her lying down and the vet was coming and going, but eventually he said he could do no more and he would have to put her down.

In those days the kennels took any dead stock off the farm and so they came the next morning. But Charlie had turned up already and he said to us *"You two be off down the field with foal...."* Then after an hour or so he came to call us back and the stable was quite fresh – he'd cleaned it all out and it was knee deep in new straw with hay and water in the corner. He was a good friend to us was Charlie.

One night, Charlie heard noises from the pool, where he found a chap trying to drown a dog. Next morning, Charlie told us all about it:
"I got the dog out, and as the man went to climb out of the pool, I pushed the bastard back into the water - about four or five times. Then I took him and the dog up to the Police Station."

During the war, when Charlie was working at Guarlford Court, an aircraft came down in The Old Seeds. Charlie ran over to see what was going on and found the pilot trapped in the aircraft. The navigator was down in the ditch because there was live ammo flying in all directions. Anyway, Charlie couldn't get the pilot out and he told us:
"The whole bloody lot had to come out, so I ripped out seat, pilot and all and got them down in the ditch. The old woodman was standing behind the hedge shouting 'Keep 'em down Charlie!' – not realising that he could have got shot himself!"
Sixty years later, the pilot's son came over to see Charlie from Australia and presented Charlie with his father's wallet as a momento.

One Sunday we went over to 'Archer's Stud' to see Charlie and Do.
"Come in and have a drink!" he said - and in our innocence we did. Anyway, we had a drink and then Charlie said to me: *"Now, I've got a drop of brandy that'll just suit you........"*.
Well, it laid me out and I slept on the lawn the whole afternoon, much to Joan's annoyance. Next time I saw Charlie he wanted to know how I was, laughing his head off. He told me the 'brandy' had been carrot whisky and that it had even laid the dustman out!

The next time I went to see him, he was having a drink and wanted me to join him.
"Have a drop of whisky kid". But I knew better by then.
"Well, you give me the bottle, Charlie," I said, which he did, and I poured my own. So I was doing alright, until a little later he suddenly turned round and pointed to the end wall.
"Now you just look at that picture over there, Joan" - and of course I fell for it and when I turned back round I found my glass full! I was sitting near the bookcase, so I hid my glass behind it......

When I left I saw Do and told her what I'd done and where I'd hidden it. We had a good laugh about it.
"I'll see to it kid - the silly old fool."

Years ago, Joan's mother was very ill in bed at Grange Farm. One day the day nurse was late and Mrs.B. had to be turned over in her bed, but Joan and I just couldn't do it. Charlie was there, working on the farm, and so I went back to join him in whatever we were doing at the time. I mentioned to Charlie about the nurse being late and he said that he'd help turn Mrs.B. over. So back to the house we went and in went Charlie, who took his cap off, respectful, as Charlie was.
"Morning, Mrs.B. maam, I've come to turn you over."
"Oh – I shall enjoy that!" she replied.
So between us we managed to get her turned over, and got her comfortable. As we were walking back to the fields, Charlie and I were talking about it.
"You don't have to worry about men & women at times like that, do you kid."

Pure gold was Charlie.

But then he was always one for 'pranks', was Charlie. Once, young Richard Newson and a friend were over at Guarlford Court, playing the men up and making a right bother of themselves. Charlie tied their bikes up in the roof of the barn, well out of their reach!
On another occasion, at one of the wartime dances, he and his pals released some mice to run about all over the floor – and of course pandemonium broke out!!!

Charlie would always call you *"kid"* and two of his frequent expressions were:
"I turned round kid and ......" But Charlie never 'swapped' anything, he'd say
"I chopped this for that...."

So I'm quite sure when he reaches the Pearly Gates he'll want to 'chop' St. Peter for something - and then he'll turn round and he'll....... Well, they'll know he's arrived, anyway!

But that was Charlie – a good friend who liked a joke and a laugh, and who'd never say no. One of nature's gentlemen, he was.

Appendix 4
NURSERYMAN & GARDEN CENTRE
15th August 1994

A FAMILY SHOW WORTH SEEING

Carol Nicholls' involvement with her nursery goes right back to her schooldays, as David Askham found out when he went to Malvern.

GRANGE FARM NURSERY IS A FAMILY business which was originally owned and run by two ladies who have since retired. Carol Nicholls recalls working part-time at the nursery, at the tender age of fifteen, weeding. She eventually became so interested in the business that she started training in horticulture at Pershore College. In 1980, after one year at college and with help from her parents, Carol bought Grange Farm Nursery. She confesses: "I just love displaying and selling good plants and I enjoy people coming into the nursery and getting to know them."

The nursery is tucked away in a corner of Guarlford village, way off the beaten track east of the Malvern Hills. It is located in one of the most delightfully converted former farmyards you are likely to find. "When we first took over the nursery there were horses in the stables. Since then the site has been slowly developed, the yard was gravelled over and the main plant displays were laid down."

It is a small plot, possibly no bigger than three-quarters of an acre and much of the space is occupied by old farm buildings; but even they have been pressed into full use and have been converted to nursery roles. An open tithe barn accommodates seasonal stock such as bedding plants, not a mainstream line but sought after by customers in season. The nursery office nestles in a stable, while the old Tack Shed has been converted into an information centre which has a good range of reference material, instructional leaflets and point-of-sale boards. Carol has a policy of not displaying point-of-sale material in the plant display area. She much prefers that plants take visual priority

The major drawback of such a small site is that there is little space for car parking, a factor which influences the timing of wholesale deliveries of new plants. Carol has to plan for new stock to arrive between 8am and 9am. When her small on-site car-park is full with clients' cars, others can park outside in the village lane.

"There are just four of us who work here, each in charge of a specific area. We work shifts, two people on each day. We don't hide away in the greenhouse: we are out here all the time, even if it is pouring with rain, keeping the plants tidy and in good condition. In addition my mother, father and husband help – but they are unpaid! There is a lot of work, particularly when the weather is windy. It is most important to keep the hot-spot plants looking good. Lois Crump, my sister-in-law, has a real talent for presenting plants and she is in charge of the acers and main displays at the shows and in the nursery. She designs our show exhibits and has an incredible skill for arranging our stand."

Horticultural shows have proved to be an important source of new business. Had it not been for their annual exhibits at the Three Counties Spring Show at Malvern, Carol Nicholls' little nursery might well have remained relatively obscure, known only to

NURSERYMAN & GARDEN CENTRE 15 AUGUST 1994

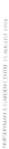

Far left – We are family! Carol Nicholls and her sister-in-law Lois Crump, who is charge of the nursery's main displays, put together a joint presentation.

Left – The climbing rose 'Maigold' glows above a spread of hostas.

more small ones than if they were displayed by themselves. One problem we face is that customers often want to buy the mature specimens. We have to explain that we need them as show plants. However, if I can get bigger plants on special order, I take the customer's name and address and advise them by postcard when the plant is available."

One effective plant group consisted of lavender 'Hidcote' purple) and Nemesia denticulata 'Confetti' with a two-year old plant of the latter dominating the display. When the plants have finished their main flowering, they are returned to the A-to-Z beds.

Each year Carol and her team tackle a new project. "This year we invested in a computer for the business. Last year we established a woodland garden with associated plants, specialising in Japanese maples, which are very popular.

"We sell a lot of camellias, fruit and ornamental trees. Roses are obtained mainly from David Austin and are looking in very fine condition now they are in flower. We have a big bulk order of bare-root roses in the autumn and we pot them and grow them on ourselves. This gives us additional work in the quiet winter months."

A lot of pre-ordered hanging baskets are made up by the nursery in an old cattle shed. They use a wide choice of plants and herb baskets featured for the first time this year

Carol Nicholls does not envisage moving the nursery to a bigger site because she likes it where it is. An expanding business would need more staff and she fears that she would lose her all-important personal involvement.

Throughout the country there are probably many more smaller nurseries like Grange Farm Nursery than those which operate in the big league. Provided they are run in the thoroughly professional and refreshing way that Carol Nicholls and her small team practise in her nursery, the public at large will continue to be well served by the plant nurseries industry.

Some of the nursery's plant display beds, with the old stables in the background.

local people There is little scope for significant natural expansion to her business, but she recognised something was amiss when even her regular customers failed to turn up when the Malvern Flower Show proved to be a bigger attraction. So, six years ago, she decided to become an exhibitor at the Spring show and was delighted when her little business won a coveted RHS Silver Medal. The next year she was awarded a Silver-Gilt medal. Since then, she has attended the Spring show every year and has been rewarded with a RHS Gold Medal on each occasion.

"We learned a lot from our first show and gradually built in improvements. The public like to see how young plants will grow. So we decided to produce some fine specimen plants which we could display on our stand. These made all the difference and certainly contributed to our successes at Malvern The ensuing publicity brought the nursery to the attention of a wider group of gardeners and visitors now come from much further afield, many from Gloucester and Cheltenham. Our aim is to attract the more discerning gardeners who are looking for something special for their gardens."

A striking feature of the plant sales area is the way that mature trees have been retained rather than being swept away to make more space. There's an old climbing rose 'Maigold', which also contributes to the sense of maturity and a pleasant atmosphere.

"We try to group plants, like our hollies, into specific areas. I don't have just one holly, but as many different species as I can find. It is the same with ferns. We have to use our limited space as productively as possible and we have found that one large plant will help sell many

Appendix 5

TELEGRAPH GARDENING
5TH February, 2005

Nurseryoftheweek

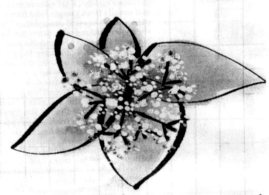

Viburnum tinus 'eve price'

Grange Farm Nursery, on the edge of the picturesque Malvern Hills, specialises in ornamental shrubs and trees, with the emphasis on low-maintenance plants for busy people. The outstanding quality and breadth of the range, which includes many AGM-holders, is a testament to owner Carol Nicholl's devotion and skill.

Nicholl began working here as a schoolgirl in 1975, then went on to train at Pershore College, before returning to buy the business in 1980. At the height of winter, when most nurseries tend to look untidy and unkempt, Grange Farm is still fresh and inviting, with arrangements of variegated evergreens, silver-leafed and winter-flowering shrubs and fruitful plants. These themed collections offer inspiration for seasonal planting and change throughout the year. The ranges are laid out alphabetically, so gardeners with a wishlist can find their desired plants easily. Nicholl and her staff are happy to offer advice. Grange Farm has no catalogue or mail order .

Val Bourne

Grange Farm Nursery, Guarlford, Malvern, Worcestershire WR13 6NT (01684 562544). No mail order or catalogue. Open daily: 9am-5.30pm (or dusk), Monday to Saturday; 10am-4.30pm Sunday.

Appendix 6

THE LADY
25th March 2008

THE CONSTANT
GARDENER

Despite the forebodings of her schoolteachers, Carol Nicholls took on the management of a plant nursery when she was just 20, and has since won many medals. **Diana Hutchinson** learns how she plotted her flourishing career

Carol Nicholls cannot remember a day when she was not besotted by plants. The purple clematis 'Jackmanii' that used to weave its way up and round the walls of her childhood home near Southampton, the shrubs in the garden, even the potatoes her father grew in an allotment behind their house, seemed just magical.

"I loved helping my father dig up the potatoes. I couldn't wait to get out into the garden," she says. "I can't tell you who my school friends were, but I loved our plants and I remember them still."

On Sundays the family used to visit *The Yellow Book* gardens (those that open for charity under the auspices of the National Gardens Scheme). Not exactly typical entertainment for the usual eight-year-old, but Carol was in her element. She was glad when the family left the busy south of England for Malvern, in the farming county of Worcestershire. Her father, a chief planning officer, took a house on an old road beside one of the open commons.

"It was like moving to paradise," recalls Carol. "I had the Malvern Hills to walk on and greenery all round me."

In her snug office in the converted stables of Grange Farm Nursery in Guarlford, overlooking the hills, there are gardeners' fleeces in every colour hanging on pegs. Carol's, in clematis purple, is on the back of an old swivel chair. Through the open door I catch a glimpse of spring flowers – purple cyclamen, miniature daffodils and the waft of blue hyacinth scent.

Carol took over as boss of the nursery when she was just 20, even though her school had poured cold water on the idea of a girl getting her hands dirty.

"I passed A-level geography and biology, but I knew what I wanted to do," she says. "When I told the careers teacher that I wanted to study horticulture she pooh-poohed it. It was not considered the done thing then, particularly for a grammar school pupil. Certainly not for a girl."

Luckily, Carol's father, John Tozer, could see the potential for garden centres and knew his daughter had set her heart on working in a nursery.

On one of her parents' *Yellow Book* trips, they drove past Guarlford and saw a nursery on a corner opposite the church. A long path led up to a small, picture-book-perfect farmhouse.

"I thought I'd go and see if I could get a job," Carol says. "I was invited to become a Saturday girl for 40p an hour. I jumped

1. **Carol and the winning clematis at the Malvern Spring Gardening Show, 2007**
2. **Foliage plants appear to their best advantage in this display at the nursery**
3. **Six months after buying Guarlford in 1980 Carol, aged 20, oversees her acres**
4. **Her daughter Rowena, who is now 21**

at the chance. I knew at once – I can't explain how that I wanted to be part of this nursery for ever."

The farm and nursery were run by two former Land Army girls, Miss Joan Bradshaw and Miss Joan Newell, who became friends during the Second World War. Like Carol, they fell in love with the outdoor life and took up farming, mainly dairy, but by 1975 they were experiencing hard times and were using part of their land to sell garden plants.

"On my first day, my job was weeding under an oak tree. It was only a seedling but it set off to grow mightily. I kept that tree for years because it reminded me of my first job."

While Carol learned the ropes, she was put on the till, serving the customers.

"I was so nervous! I hated taking money, and giving change was even worse. I had to write the sum down so I could see it. Luckily, people round here are lovely and were very kind to me.

"There were reference books here and if there was something I didn't know about a plant, I looked it up. I found that once I picked up the plant and touched it, looked at the leaves and its shape, I had learned it."

In no time she was working through school holidays. Nursery life, particularly the business side, was taking hold of her. The two Joans offered her a full-time job and she was sent on a day-release scheme to nearby Pershore College to study horticulture. Two years later, the Joans decided to retire. They wanted the nursery to progress, but they needed a buyer. Carol could not bear the idea that Grange Farm might be taken from her. She turned to her father. Would he back her?

"He said, yes, we'd do it," she recalls. "I was lucky that everyone trusted me. The two Joans had faith in me and let me buy the land. They were two women who had made a success of farming at a time

when it was a male prerogative and they allowed a girl of 20 a chance, too.

"I never felt frightened that I would let Dad down. It might have been the confidence of youth and naïvety but I knew how to sell a plant and I knew I had to sell them."

Carol never bought a plant that was not hardy, and suited to the local climate. She never bought a plant unless it was coming into leaf or bloom, so customers could see what they were getting. She also knew to display it where it would sell, so she built a picture by making miniature gardens, putting bright-coloured plants together to show each other off. It made the nursery more like a garden in bloom, with many points of drama.

Customers came but, just as Carol was congratulating herself for always finishing the week in profit, disaster struck.

"It was January 1982, there were days of frost and then one night the temperature fell to minus 25. Great chunks of ice like floating glaciers jammed the River Severn around Worcester. I lost 50% of the stock. Some plants were frozen for so long the roots had rotted. All the hebes and escallonias were wiped out. At least I know now which plants must be covered and we have overcoats for them all."

As the cold went on, Carol realised the

disaster had hit the surrounding gardens and, come the spring, customers would need replacement plants. So, she went off to Devon and Somerset with her father to source and buy stock. Carol's mother, Shirley, as well as her father, helped her build up the nursery, and they still go in to give a hand. Her husband, Rollin, works alongside her, and their two daughters, Rowena, 21, and Ashley, 18, have both been Saturday girls.

Over the years, the former Saturday girl, who dreamed of a life spent working with plants, has won a row of Royal Horticultural Society medals – golds and silver gilts among them – at the celebrated Malvern Spring Gardening Show. Last year, however, she scooped the jackpot.

John Richards, who runs a local wholesale nursery, invited her to launch a new black clematis. Carol agreed and sought the help of her sister-in-law, Lois, on how best to display the very dark purple flowers of clematis 'Purple Rain' in the subdued lighting of a marquee.

Lois introduced a mass of 'Broughton Bride', a white clematis, at the back of their stand and Carol brought the black clematis forward so that the visitors could see it. She was awarded not only a gold medal but Best in Show, too.

Her husband was on the stand to see her triumph. He has been so enthused by Carol's love of plants that some time ago he gave up his family business to retrain at Pershore College on a three-year course.

"Now he knows much more than I do," she declares cheerfully. ☙

● The Malvern Spring Gardening Show runs from 8 to 11 May. For tickets call 01684-584924 (www.threecounties.co.uk/springgardening).
● Grange Farm Nursery, Guarlford, Malvern, Worcestershire WK13 6NT (01684-562544).

Appendix 7

WORCESTERSHIRE LIFE

July 2010

It's all about the Gardens

Twenty five years ago a converted cattle shed hosted the first Malvern Spring Gardening Show. Today, it's one of the biggest, and best, shows on the gardening calendar. Debbie Graham toured the gardens and floral marquees to find out why Malvern is so special.

INSIDE THE FLORAL MARQUEE

Carol Nichols of Grange Farm Nursery, Malvern, Worcestershire

Carol's A Journey in Time garden had the whole showground talking as it won not just a coveted RHS Gold Medal but also bagged the People's Choice Award, voted for by visitors.

"We could not have wished for more, or done any better," says Carol who has been coming to the show for the last 24 years and was one of the 25 nurseries that chose to incorporate the show's silver anniversary into their display.

A picture perfect, romantic garden was the result with a clock taking centre stage to symbolise the passing of time and the Show's coloured gates are mirrored in the design.

Carol's secret is simple:

"It is the combinations of these easy-to-grow plants that is important," she says. "You can make a picture in your garden by doing it the right way.

"The nicest comment we had from somebody yesterday was that we had inspired her to do something with her own garden and she has become a gardener. I think that is the nicest thing."

Orchids by Peter White, Banbury, Oxfordshire

For gold medal winner Peter making the journey from Oxford to the show is an annual event.

"We always come to Malvern as we have a lot of friends in the area," he says. "This is my favourite show because the people are so friendly. I love coming here; it is the best show on the calendar."

Winning gold medals here is becoming something of a habit – this is his third at Malvern.

The display took him a day and a half to put together and for him the bad winter weather was a

Lois Speedy and Carol Nicholls – Grange Farm Nursery, Malvern.

HRH The Princess Royal tours the show in th company of Mike Warner.

Craig Hamilton-Smith in the Morgan Garden.

Emilio De Beer, Fuchsiavale Nurseries (Torton, Kidderminster).

blessing: "It's done us a favour as the big flowers at the bottom of the display have flowered later, normally they have finished by now."

Emilio De Beer of Fuchsiavale Nurseries, Kidderminster Worcestershire

This stunning display of around 70-80 fuchsias was put together by 19-year-old grandson of the nursery's founders, Emilo, with the help of a colleague.

This was his first RHS show, although Fuchsiavale have been at Malvern ever since the beginning, and was thrilled to get a silver gilt medal.

"Fuchsias need warmth and light to come into flower and this year we had such a long and dull winter that we were struggling, so a silver gilt was a great achievement."

So what are his plans for the future?

"This has left me in a bit of a dilemma because I love what I do but I am due to go to university this September to study sports science." So sports science's loss may be horticulture's gain.

IN THE SHOW GARDENS

Craig Hamilton-Smyth, designe of 'The Morgan Garden' sponsored by the Morgan Motor Company.

Craig, nephew of Charles Morgan, designed a show garden of contrast with both the iconic Morgan car an wild flowers at its heart. and was awarded a silver medal.

"I love wild flowers you can't real beat nature. It always looks fantastic," he says.

But the garden is really about highlighting Morgan's commitmen to the environment.

The Information

INDEPENDENT

The essential guide for going out and staying in 10.03.2012

Garden centres

offering advice and gar... tips is worth keeping an eye for sensible, monthly updat... **Where** Weybourne Rd, Kelling, Holt, Norfolk, NR25 7ER (01263 711574; emcy.co.uk)

21 Grange Farm Nursery
Extremely helpful and knowledgeable plantswomen run this nursery near Malvern. It specialises in camellias which can be fussy flowers. There is no cafe or gift shop as this place prides itself on being a proper nursery for proper gardeners. If you want a water feature go somewhere else.
Where Guarlford, Malvern, Worcestershire, WR13 6NT (01684 562544)

Appendix 9

INSTITUTE OF
ADVANCED MOTORISTS

This is to Certify that

Jo Newell

*has passed the Advanced Driving Test
and has been elected a Member of the*

Institute of Advanced Motorists

Vice President:
J.M. ROBOTHAM, O.B.E., F.C.A.

Chairman:
JOHN H. MAXWELL, C.A.

MEMBERSHIP Nº **339945**
DATE **15. 10. 2005**

*This Certificate does not authorise the holder
to give professional tuition for the Institute's
Driving Test*

Chief Executive:
CHRISTOPHER T. BULLOCK, B.Sc., F.R.S.A.

Bibliography

The Guarlford Story	Guarlford History Group	Pub.	GHG	2005
The Guarlford Scene	Guarlford History Group	Pub.	GHG	2008
The Outer Cabinet	G.Dudley	Pub.	GCDA	2008
CJKB	John Bradshaw	Unpublished		2007

Appx.1
Memories of Wartime Service Jo Newell
Lioness ATC Comrades Ass'n Vol.85, No.2 2009

Appx.2
Worcestershire Memories Peter Henshaw
Tractor Magazine August 2009

Appx. 4
A Family Show Worth Seeing David Askham
Nurseryman & Garden Centre magazine 15.09.1994

Appx.5
Nursery of the Week Val Bourne
Telegraph Gardening 05/02/2005

Appx.6
The Constant Gardener Diana Hutchinson
The Lady 25/03/2008

Appx.7
It's All About Gardening Debbie Graham
Worcestershire Life July 2010

Appx.8
The 50 Best Garden Centres
The Independent 10.03.2012

Amenuensis and Editor

John Bradshaw is often referred to by others, and sometimes by Jo Newell herself, as being her nephew, which is neither true nor insulting, hopefully for both parties.

In fact, for the first third of his life the *Two Joans* were called *"Auntie Joan"* and *"Auntie Jo"*, until he became a student and was taller than his real aunt, whereupon it was suggested that just plain *"Joan"* and *"Jo"* would do. Away from Guarlford, however, they were referred to as *"... my great aunts!"* or latterly *"... my Aged Aunts..."*

John's professional life was spent working with and writing about mathematics and education, editing a mathematics journal and organising conferences & workshops whilst teaching in schools, college and university. He has also written books and many articles concerning mathematics, education and motoring.

However, upon retirement, he embarked upon his first biography, that of his father, Colin, which expanded beyond all expectations and inevitably included much about his sister, John's aunt, and Jo Newell's partner, Joan Bradshaw. While there were necessarily many references to Jo too, it did not begin to do justice to her life, and hence this book was written.

It was all started by Jo herself when she was asked to give a talk to the Guarlford W.I. about her life in the Army. This went down so well that she was asked back to talk about local farming just after the war and then about the creation of the new nursery. Trumpet W.I. then also asked her to give talks and fortunately they were recorded and so when this book was proposed, Gill Ferris transcribed them to form the core of this book. It too then expanded beyond all expectations.....

John Bradshaw currently lives in both the Scottish Borders and Malvern, but also travels a great deal.

Also by JRB:

Square Forum (with Ralph Hawkins)
Mathematics and Art (with Leslie Jones)
Ariels and Their Owners
CJKB – a biography of Colin Bradshaw
Transmogrification
A Tall Short Story
The Artful Bodger (with Peter Henshaw)
ODTAA